The Extraordinary UnOrdinary You

FOLLOW YOUR OWN PATH,
DISCOVER YOUR OWN JOURNEY

YOU

*The*
*Extraordinary*
*UnOrdinary*

SIMONE KNEGO

**LIONCREST**

PUBLISHING

THE EXTRAORDINARY UNORDINARY YOU

*Follow Your Own Path, Discover Your Own Journey*

ISBN   978-1-5445-0934-1 *Hardcover*

978-1-5445-0933-4 *Paperback*

978-1-5445-0932-7 *Ebook*

*To my mom, my sister, my daughters, and all of the women in this world who strive to be "enough." We're more than enough. We're Extraordinary.*

# CONTENTS

# INTRODUCTION

"SERIOUSLY? No, you can't have ice cream before breakfast! It's not your birthday."

This sentence perfectly sums up the story of my everyday life—and maybe yours too—a never-ending cycle of meal preparation, house cleaning, homework help, and shuttling back and forth from every corner of the city and beyond. I am in the thick of cheering, prodding, feeding, and sometimes even scolding—all day long. My life is at times exhausting but never dull.

When people learn I have six children, they might say, "How do you do it? You're extraordinary." But I honestly have never seen myself as extraordinary. I am your basic, ordinary, everyday mother trying to keep up with the laundry. And through it all, I never feel that I am doing enough because there is always more to do.

But, in my everyday, run-of-the-mill life, I have had these extraordinary moments where I've been faced with a choice—the choice to step up and do something meaningful, or to look the other way and let the opportunity pass me by. More often than not, I've made the choice to step up, simply because it was the right thing to do. I believe that each of us has the same kind of moments. If we choose to step up and act in those moments, those moments begin to shape and define our lives. And in these moments, even the most basic person like me is able to do extraordinary things.

One of those moments came while I was sitting in a women's empowerment luncheon. It was one of those aha moments that come in a flash, but the effects linger on. There were two amazing, inspirational speakers who told us their stories of being self-made. One was a woman who quit her day job and created multiple companies that were now valued at over $200 million dollars. The other speaker was equally as accomplished. I sat there in awe, so impressed by their achievements. I looked around the room and everyone seemed to feel the same way. But as I got up to leave, I truly questioned if I was inspired, or if I felt a little bit bad about myself.

Yes—these women were inspiring—but I'll never be them. And I'll probably never achieve anything close to what they've achieved.

Then, in a stroke of what only can be called inspiration, a thought flashed into my mind. That's the whole point—you don't have to be anybody but who you actually are. You just need to realize that what you do every day inspires the people around you to be the best they can be. If you change the way you see yourself, the world around you will change.

That day was a turning point for me—a realization that I just needed to be me. I don't need to compare myself to anyone else. I'm capable of inspiring the people around me just as I am. And with that realization, I saw the world around me through a different lens. Sure, I still see myself in the mirror every morning and need to remind myself of what I'm capable of. I truly believe even the most inspirational women, the women people aspire to be like, probably still do the same. But now when I look in the mirror I can see me rather than hope for the reflection of someone I wish I could be.

**HAPPILY UNBALANCED**

Being a mother has been one of my greatest blessings of life, and an important part of my journey. It hasn't always been easy, but it has always been worth it. Motherhood is not all of me—but it is a major part.

My journey also includes those things that I do outside of the home to contribute to the world around me. I have always believed that it is important for me to use my skills and talents to contribute to the world, and to our family, in a positive way. For me, I have been able to accomplish this through both professional employment and meaningful volunteer work. I'm constantly searching for balance in my happily unbalanced life.

As a mother, it's important for me to set a good example for my children in both my personal and professional life. Through my work outside the home, they are able to see that they can do whatever they set their mind to, and that we all have something to contribute to this world. I feel that by making my own contribution to the world, it makes me a better mother, and it allows me to use my brain and my skills for things outside of being a mom.

I've also found much fulfillment in the volunteer work I've done. As a co-chair of the National Young Leadership for the Jewish Federation of North America, I've had the great honor of working side by side with some of the most amazing leaders, learning from them, and being inspired by them. The choices I've made have led to extraordinary adventures.

Every journey is like that. It's our choices that are the guiding factor.

## *TIKKUM OLAM*—REPAIR THE WORLD

Growing up in the Jewish community has been an important part of my journey, and it has helped me to see that the world is a very big place. Some of my Jewish friends were very Orthodox, and others were more secular, with a strong commitment to the customs and traditions. My family was more about the customs and traditions, which is what Rob and I focus on in our own family. To me, Judaism isn't just about being religious—we aren't a religious family. It's about being part of a community whose fundamental values are centered around family and making the world a better place for everyone in it.

Being a member of the Jewish community also reminds me often that there's still so much we can do to care for the people in it. One of the most important aspects of Judaism, for me, is the concept of *Tikkun Olam*, which means "repair the world." It doesn't just mean to repair the Jewish world—it's about repairing the whole world, and really looking at the world from a different perspective. Our behaviors and actions should be beneficial to the world around us.

In the Jewish community, we simply want to take care of people. I volunteer with the Jewish Federation because it is an organization that does exactly that. There are many organizations within the Jewish community who are doing their best to be the good in the world. Many of the funds that we contribute to the community are for programs, including the local food bank. It isn't just for Jewish people, but for all people. Our goal is to reach out and help all humanity—to make the world a better place for all of us. It's not about religion; it's about people and the good we all can do for each other.

## THE WORLD NEEDS HEALING

As I write this book, we're in the middle of a global pandemic, protests are spreading like flames throughout our country to fight racial injustice, and the need to serve one another has never been greater. Like everyone else, I'm navigating situations and making choices that I never thought I would have to face. With the events of COVID-19, everything has changed, and we've changed as a people. Life will never be what it once was. Social distancing has become a new catchphrase, and masks are no longer just for bandits and superheroes.

My aunt died from COVID-19. She lived an amazing ninety-four years, but she died alone. My husband is a neurosurgeon and continues to work. Emergencies don't stop during a pandemic, and therefore he can't stop. He washes his hands so much they feel like leather. When he gets home at the end of the day, he strips down in the garage, sprays everything with Lysol, and heads right to the shower. He's worried that he'll carry the virus home with him. He's scared because we have a child with an autoimmune disorder, and she is immunosuppressed.

COVID-19 has reminded us that we may not be able to control what's happening in our world, but we can control how we respond to what's happening. I always try to look for the silver lining. I'm not saying that I don't have moments when I feel completely unmotivated or sad because of the pandemic or the current state of our world—I'm human. But when those moments happen, I think about my blessings. I focus on the little things I can do to make myself feel better.

For me, those little things usually involve spending time with family and reaching out and helping others. Bringing supplies to elderly neighbors and masks to coworkers, calling my mom everyday so that we know she's okay, and giving what we can—even when we're unsure of our own financial future. We need to support one another. We must stop comparing our lives today to life as we planned it so we can embrace the life that's waiting for us.

This time at home under quarantine has made me realize those things that are truly important to me. From this part of our family story, I want our kids to remember the quality time we've been given together. We sit down at the dinner table every night, and the kids actually eat what I have cooked. My house has never been cleaner, and all of my kids now know how to wash their own clothes, mop the floor, and scrub toilets. Most importantly, I have all of my kids back under one roof for at least the next few months. Although these have been extremely challenging times for all of us, in many ways, I am thankful for this "pause" we have experienced.

Our dinner table has been filled with impassioned conversations about what's happening in the world around us. We are honest with our kids and encourage them to ask the difficult questions because that is what we are there for—to love them and educate them. We have discussed the importance of wearing masks, not only to prevent the spread of the virus, but to demonstrate respect for other people. We've emphasized the criticality of data and research and the need to truly educate ourselves on a subject before giving input or spreading information. And we have discussed the importance of respecting someone's opinion, even when it conflicts with our own.

So many people post on social media, berating others for taking precautions due to the pandemic. Trust me. We understand and feel the financial effects of the economic shutdown. But as a physician's family, we also see and hear firsthand accounts of how devastating and deadly the COVID-19 virus has and will continue to be. The need for kindness and respect cannot be overemphasized.

## ORDINARY LIFE, EXTRAORDINARY MOMENTS

I'm not a licensed therapist, nor am I an expert on life. I'm just a woman on a journey that, so far, has taught me some remarkable things. Even this pandemic has taught me lessons and brought about changes in my life that have made me better than I was coming into it. But like every experience that's come before it, this pandemic is another stop on my journey to becoming my best self.

It's in finding my own path, and discovering my own journey, that I have been given these extraordinary moments that have shaped my life and defined my mission. We all have these extraordinary moments. But sometimes, we fail to see them as extraordinary. It took me a long time to change the way I saw myself and the world around me.

Many people think that what they do in life isn't really that important. They look at other people who they view as truly making a difference—people who have created foundations that save lives, philanthropists who invest in people and do so much good in the world, or volunteers who sacrifice their time in far-off countries—and they wish they could be more like them. But most people don't have the option to leave whatever they are doing to help someone halfway around the world. That just isn't everyone's reality.

If anything, this pandemic is a reminder that you don't have to travel the world to make a difference in it. What you need to realize is that what you are doing right where you are—in your own corner of the world—is making just as big of an impact. The things you do every day are making a difference.

Looking at everyone and measuring our accomplishments or failures to theirs is a backward way of looking at life. Forget about what other people are doing, and look at all the good YOU can do. Stop wasting your time and energy, thinking to yourself, "I'll never be able to do that!" Figure out what you can do, then go and do it.

During this worldwide pandemic, some people sang on their balconies in solidarity, and others sewed masks. There were people of every religion who came together and fasted and prayed for relief, while others jeopardized their own welfare to serve on the frontlines in the hospitals, grocery stores, and other essential jobs. So many figured out what they could do, and they did it, no questions asked.

Let's take the lessons we've learned from this pandemic and apply them even after it's over. Life is full of opportunities to touch the lives of those around you, and it can begin right where you are, today. You'll never regret the choice to do something good, even for a perfect stranger. I don't think I've ever heard of a time when someone has regretted doing something kind for someone else. Most people are just the opposite, because doing good brings more feelings of good.

To me, the definition of success is not how much money

you have in your bank account or how popular you are. To me, the definition of success is happiness. It's your family, and it's the impact you have on the world around you, right where you are. It's about being a good person, and the best YOU that you can be.

In this book, I don't just want to inspire you to go out there and be the good. I want you to realize that you're already doing good in your everyday life—you simply need to recognize it. Just because your journey to change the world doesn't take you to a far-off country, doesn't mean you aren't making a difference right where you are. I really want to emphasize this point, which to me is the heart and soul of this book.

I'm not here to tell you how to live your life, but I am here to tell you that you are UnOrdinary, simply because you are you. You are Extraordinary in the everyday things that you do. And above all, you have your own path to find and your own journey to discover. It is my hope that by sharing my experiences with you, you will feel inspired to discover your own journey. There's no time like the present. The world is waiting for the Extraordinary, UnOrdinary You!

## FINDING OUR MISSING PIECES

Everyone struggles. You're going to have many days when life is hard and you are struggling to keep things together. Believe me—I have plenty of those days myself.

But even in the struggle, there are lessons that can be found in the journey. I remind myself of this everyday—be in the moment, learn from the experience.

My journey has taken me all around the world and back again. In every country I've visited, there's always something that I bring back with me—a memory, an experience, a souvenir for the kids.

But the greatest gift the world has given me is my children. Every time we brought a child home, our family felt more complete. Our first three children were brought home from the hospital. Our last three children were brought home from South Korea and Africa. In bringing them home, we weren't trying to rescue children; we were looking for our family's missing pieces, and halfway across the world, we found them. They didn't come all at once, but together, they made our family whole.

*Chapter 1*

# THE VIRTUE OF PATIENCE

## LEARNING THE "KOREAN WAY"

Some of my greatest lessons in patience have come from being a mother.

We adopted Noah from South Korea when he was just four months old. When we made the decision to adopt, even our closest friends questioned our choice.

"You can have more biological kids right? So, why not just have another one?"

We just explained to our friends that there were so many kids out there simply waiting for a family to love them, and we wanted to be one of those families.

In most cases, when you apply to adopt a child, you don't get to just pick any child—you're actually matched with a child. Once you're matched, you're sent a photo and information regarding the child they matched you with. When we got that first photo of Noah, it was a beautiful picture of him in a white gown, but my eyes were drawn to the number on a small sign placed over the gown he was wearing. That's all that identified him. He was K06-410, just a number. When our friends saw the picture, they finally understood why this was so important to us.

When it was time to go to South Korea to pick Noah up, Rob stayed home with our girls, Emma and Olivia, while I made the trip with Jacob. Jacob was only ten at the time, but he really grew up on that trip and was such a big help to me.

We had already been in Seoul for three days before we actually had the opportunity to meet Noah. We explored the capital city by subway, visited some of the most exquisite Buddhist temples, and even had enough time to enjoy Lotte World Theme Park. We really didn't sleep much because of the massive time difference—twelve hours.

We arrived at the adoption agency office in Seoul on day four not knowing what to expect. As we walked into the office, I was so nervous. Jacob and I sat down and waited anxiously. When the door finally opened, my jitters went away as I saw Noah's beautiful face and chubby cheeks. He was even more handsome in person than in the photos we had received of him.

Noah's foster mom was so sweet with Noah, and we could tell that she really loved him. She had fostered nearly forty children, and I'm sure she loved them all. As she put him into my arms, tears flowed down her cheeks. She kissed him and quickly said goodbye. My heart ached for both of them. I knew she had taken care of many babies, but her tears showed how much she really cared for him.

Once all the paperwork was completed, we were able to take Noah and start our journey home. It took us an hour by taxi to get to our hotel, and Noah was screaming at the top of his lungs the entire time. No matter what we tried, we couldn't get him to stop crying. Even the poor taxi driver was trying to calm Noah down by shaking his keys. But Noah would not be comforted.

In the hotel room, Noah didn't like the bassinet, so Jacob offered to hold him. It didn't bother Jacob at all that Noah was screaming. He just held him and started flipping through the channels on the TV. A baseball game came on, and all of a sudden, Noah went silent.

Jacob and I just looked at each other in awe. We had no idea what had happened, but we knew that the baseball game was staying on.

The next morning, with no more than two hours of sleep, we packed up for our flight home, with Noah crying all the while. I honestly couldn't figure it out. I kept thinking to myself, "I've done this three times before. I should be able to quiet a baby!" I already had three kids, and I thought I was doing pretty well. But maybe I overestimated my mothering abilities; I felt so discouraged.

If you are anything like me, life has a way of making you really question yourself when a choice you've made doesn't end up looking like the picture you had in your head.

I really started questioning myself and my life choices. I began to wonder if I was mentally strong enough to handle the challenges I was being faced with. But I was already all in, and I couldn't back down. We had to just keep moving forward, crying baby and all.

By the time we got to the airport, we were finally able to quiet Noah down.

"Okay, we're going to be okay," I thought.

I spent extra money and purchased a first-class seat so we could lie flat, which was one of the dumbest things I've ever done. I thought the plane would take off and Noah would fall asleep on me and we could recline and sleep through a good portion of the flight. The idea looked great inside my mind but didn't play out well in real life.

When we boarded the plane, they put the bassinet in the bulkhead area, and they strapped it in. From the second we sat down—Noah started screaming. I felt horrible. Not only was I unable to calm him down, but few people in the first-class cabin were empathetic to the situation. I carried Noah back to the galley, and literally stood there for hours on end, trying to comfort my new baby.

The people on the other side of the curtain kept pulling it open to see the mother who couldn't quiet her child. I just kept saying, "I'm really sorry. I'm trying my best here." It was one of my greatest lessons in patience.

I felt completely out of my element, and I had been a mother for over a decade! Most of the people were giving me looks—not nice looks. But some of the people peeking behind the curtain were kind and offered to help me. I just kept thinking, "What am I going to do with this poor baby? He doesn't really even know what's happening. His whole life has been changed in two seconds."

Finally, after ten hours of trying, one of the flight attendants came up and said, "Can I try the Korean way?"

Relieved, I said, "You can try whatever you like."

She took Noah in her arms, put him on his stomach, placed him on her back, and started bouncing. She was hunched over at a ninety-degree angle as she bounced. Noah's eyes started to close, and in two seconds, he was asleep.

I had no idea that there was a Korean way of quieting a baby. She could have made it up—but it worked!

## EACH CHILD IS UNIQUE

I knew how to be a mother, but this experience taught me that I needed to learn how to be Noah's mother. Talk about a humbling experience. It required patience, because I needed to learn how to be a different kind of mother to him. I think so many times in our lives, we keep doing things the same way we've always done them, not realizing that sometimes there's a better way of doing them. Change is hard. It doesn't come overnight. It's often a gradual process, taking time and a fair share of mistakes. But if we're patient with the process—and especially patient with ourselves and open to doing old things in a new way—we can do so much more.

It was a long trip to Chicago, and an even longer trip home since our flight from Chicago was canceled and we had to spend the night at the Chicago airport. We got a hotel room, but no one slept because Noah screamed the entire time.

The next day, we had two more flights to get us home. Noah

cried the entire flight from Chicago to Atlanta—big shocker. But on the flight from Atlanta to Sarasota, he maybe whimpered once. He was as worn out as I was, and probably had no energy left to get the tears out.

When we landed in Sarasota, not only were we greeted by Rob and the girls, but our friends had come with signs and posters cheering us on and welcoming us home. It was a beautiful sight to see.

When I saw Rob, it was finally my time to cry. I was emotionally spent. I handed Noah to Rob, and he held both of us in his arms. I knew that we could raise this baby together.

One of my favorite family photos is at the airport. You can tell that Noah is screaming. Rob is holding him. Emma is standing with her fingers in her ears to drown out the crying. And I look like I'm half-dead. But we made it home. We made it home.

That was the beginning of our life with Noah.

## PATIENCE IN THE TRYING MOMENTS

My experience with Noah's adoption taught me that I can't always fix things in the moment. Sometimes, I just have to roll with it. I am sure that I am not the only one who has had to try to comfort a crying baby on a long flight home, and

I am certain I won't be the last. We all have experienced circumstances that we can't control. It might not be a baby screaming for ten hours on a flight, but we've all had situations that we can't fix and things that lie outside our control. When those moments come, the only thing we can control is how we react to those situations. And oftentimes, we just have to do our best to remain levelheaded in the moment.

We have to figure out a way to make it bearable until we find the solution—because there is always some kind of solution. We just have to be patient enough to find it.

It's so easy in stressful situations to let our guard down and allow our natural response to take over. Most of the time, our first response to stressful situations comes from our human weaknesses and current emotions. But that's probably not the response any of us want to have. We're much more able to manage those situations if we are patient enough to let things play out a little more. We have to be persistently active in finding a solution, while not letting the situation get the best of us.

A lot of times, it's hard to assess things in the moment. And we are not always able to stay calm when presented with really troubling circumstances. But even if we aren't able to stay calm, cool, and collected, these experiences teach us valuable lessons. Looking back on them, we can evaluate ourselves and our reactions, recognize the wrong choices we made because we are human, and commit to do better next time. We can learn so much from our mistakes.

If we find ourselves in circumstances where the outcome is out of our control, sometimes there are things that we can do to lessen the effects on ourselves and everyone around us. I love proactive parents who, when they get on a plane for the first time with a new baby, pass everyone a note with earplugs and a lollipop attached that says, "This is my first flight. I apologize if I cry. Here are some earplugs to help you and some candy to make this flight sweeter."

I've received this cute note on a few different flights, and it really breaks the ice from the beginning. It lets people know what to expect, so when the crying does happen, people are a little less annoyed by it. But I truly believe that all the candy in the world wouldn't have made people happy on my flight home with Noah.

Sometimes you will feel that you can't control anything. There will be days when you will say to yourself, "I can't believe that just happened. And there's nothing I can do about it." When those days come, the best thing you can do for yourself is to accept what is, and move on. It's in the past—it's done. Tell yourself you're glad that it's over, and learn from it. Just move on.

When you feel that you are in a circumstance where you

have no control, it's important to remind yourself that you do have control. You may not have control of the situation, but you will always have control of how you react to it.

### PATIENCE IN DISAPPOINTMENT

We're our own biggest critics. When things go wrong, as they often do, we sometimes blame ourselves for whatever it is we lack. But in those moments of weakness, it is important that we learn how to be patient with ourselves. We may not see the end from the beginning, but we can learn to take the disappointments when they come and learn to adjust our direction when our journey doesn't take us where we had planned to go.

When my son applied to Stanford, he was devastated when the rejection letter arrived. It was heartbreaking to watch as a mother. I encouraged him to apply because I didn't ever want him to look back and say, "I wish I would have tried." I wanted him to understand that he would never know what could have been, if he didn't put himself out there in the first place. By applying, he would get either accepted or rejected. Either way, he would learn from the experience.

He did everything right when it came to his application—he had straight A's, near perfect standardized testing, meaningful volunteer work, and he even published a paper in a major medical journal. If you looked, based on requirements, he checked all the boxes and did everything he knew how to do in order to get into Stanford. But in the end, it was their decision.

Life doesn't always work out the way we want. When the rejection letter came, he had two choices: he could throw his hands up in the air and quit, or he could learn to adjust his direction. He may have lay on the floor for a while and wallowed in his sorrow, but then he chose to let go of Stanford and look for opportunities at other colleges.

Just because you feel like you deserve something, and you don't get it, doesn't mean you should stop moving forward with what you're doing. Everybody has disappointments. It's about learning to be patient with yourself as you figure out, through the disappointments, how to move forward on your journey.

My son's plan to go to Stanford didn't work out for him. He didn't get into his first-choice school. Nor did my next daughter. But they learned to make new plans. Jacob decided to attend Harvey Mudd College. The life experiences he had at Harvey Mudd changed him completely. He went from being super quiet and shy to a strong self-advocate because of the program and the people he was surrounded with. In time he realized that he ended up exactly where he was supposed to be. If he hadn't attended that school, he definitely wouldn't be the same person he is today.

Jacob was accepted at every school he applied to for grad school. Today he's at Stanford—not because they chose him, but because he chose them. In the end, my son's path to get to Stanford was totally different than what he expected. But through his patience, he was still able to get to where he wanted to go. Although his journey to Stanford began as a disappointment, it was the exact journey he needed to become the man he was meant to be.

Life is full of disappointments. But we can't let those disappointments stop us from progressing. Sometimes, we don't ever get to that place where we thought we wanted to go. If we learn to be patient with ourselves, and with our journey, life will lead us down the path that will take us exactly where we need to be.

## PATIENCE IN OUR JOURNEY

We live in a world where everything is fast-paced and instant. We want what we want now, and we struggle when we have to wait for it. We have fast-food, instant photos, streaming movies, and online shopping. All that is required is a click of the button, and the whole world is right at our fingertips.

All these instant things may bring instant pleasure, but they don't bring lasting joy—although Amazon makes me pretty happy.

Sure, there are the pleasures of life—a piece of chocolate or a walk on the beach—but these things are only pleasurable in the moment. Once they're gone, they're gone. Those things that bring happiness that lasts beyond just a single moment are things that you invest in like family, good friends, a great job, something to believe in, and something to fight for. These things require small, continuous efforts over time before you see the fruits of your labors—and the outcome is rarely immediate.

It's going to take patience and work to get anywhere worth going. Houses aren't built over night, excessive weight isn't lost after one good day of dieting, scholarships aren't awarded to just anyone. All of these things require hours and days, and maybe even years, of consistent work before the results will come.

Worthwhile things take time to grow and develop. You're one of those worthwhile things. We're often our own worst critic and we fail to see the growth we've made, and the small steps we've already taken. Change is hard, and when we take those small steps to make a change, it can be discouraging when we don't see those immediate results. We also have a tendency to see the bad things first, and they get in the way of us seeing the good. This causes us to halt our journey because we can no longer see where we're going. But by halting our journey, we also halt our progress.

We have to be patient in our journey and continue walking in the belief that the results will come. Because the moment we stop taking those steps is the moment we lose our ability to grow.

Your journey is built one piece at a time. Recognize those pieces you're building on, have patience in that journey, and remember that greater growth is the overall goal.

## PATIENCE WITH OTHERS

I had a colleague whom I worked with for two years when we co-chaired an organization together. Being a mother, I have always seen myself as a pretty patient person. With six kids, you kind of have to be. I became even more patient after working with this particular human.

We were complete opposites. He said things exactly as he saw them, and that's how he liked things done. I was a little more diplomatic in my approach. He struggled with people skills, and he knew it. It just wasn't one of his strengths. He would make a comment about something and I would have to remind him, "You can't say that." He had no filter.

One day, we were on a group call with other people on our team. We were having a heated discussion back and forth because he was moving forward on something without even asking my opinion or getting any feedback. As co-chairs, we were supposed to work as a team, and all decisions were supposed to be made together.

As I was trying to explain my frustrations, instead of listening to me, he said, in front of everyone else on the call, "Simone, you sound really upset. Why don't you go make yourself a sandwich!" Instead of trying to work with me, he invalidated my concerns and dismissed me in front of our peers by telling me to go make myself a sandwich.

Instantly, I felt anger and frustration welling up inside of me. But instead of saying what I really wanted to say to him and then promptly hanging up the phone, I thought better of it and asked myself, "Okay, how can I turn this one around?"

I took a few deep breaths, made a joke about his comment and how I was going to use that on my kids from now on when they get frustrated, and we moved on with the conference call.

I really do use that on my kids when they start arguing with me. And the funny thing is that we have made it into a joke at our house. We roll our eyes, give a snicker, and realize how silly we've been. When I tell them to go make a sandwich, it diffuses the situation and we all just start laughing.

I could have hung up the phone. I could have done a lot of

things. But instead, I made lemonade out of lemons, and now the term is something endearing in my family.

We are all different, with different approaches to life, and our journeys. There's nothing in life that's a one-size-fits-all approach. We have to have patience to be able to work with different kinds of people and the flexibility to roll with the punches. If we can learn to do that, we can actually learn from each other.

My colleague and I both had to lead with patience because we saw things from totally different perspectives. We ended up making a great team and becoming good friends. I learned so much from the time I spent working with him. He actually learned things from me, as well. At the end of our term, he thanked me for really helping to change him in certain ways. Of course, my response was, "You mean by making sandwiches?"

Even as adults who are supposedly set in our ways, we are capable of realizing that there are other ways to see things and that patience really is a virtue. It will help us to diffuse even the most difficult of circumstances and give us the ability to stop for a moment and try to see someone else's perspective.

## LOVE AND PATIENCE

Seeing things from Noah's perspective was much harder than working with an adult. Noah was a baby, and his only way to communicate was through his cries. We would ride in the car, and he would scream. We would put him in the bathtub, and he would scream. We would put him in the crib, and he would scream. If we laid him down anywhere, he would scream. But we got used to it. All we could do was simply love him.

But because we loved him, we wanted desperately to understand why he was crying. This took time and patience. Rather than get frustrated by his screaming, we started trying to understand him. It took time and a lot of trial and error. But eventually, in our process of trying and loving and trying again, we learned some things. We realized that Noah hated being on his back. He would struggle with sensory overload, and lying on his back made him miserable.

Later, Noah was diagnosed with ADHD and autism spectrum disorder. Each child with this type of diagnosis is unique and different. We've now lived with Noah long enough to understand his needs. Over the years, we've learned what situations work for Noah, and what situations are going to overwhelm him. He doesn't react negatively to be obstinate. Sometimes, he just isn't able to completely control how he feels. Now that we understand Noah, and his needs, we're able to better help him grow and thrive.

Unfortunately, the world isn't always so patient. For example, when Noah was ten, we were invited to attend an end-of-the-year pool party. Social gatherings can be difficult for Noah since he struggles with social cues, but we decided to go anyway. He was having a great time in the pool when suddenly I heard him screaming at the top of his lungs in anger. The other kids explained to me that Noah was upset because he didn't get the raft he wanted. The kids understood his struggles since they've been together since kindergarten, and it wasn't a big deal to them.

As I asked Noah to get out of the pool, I overheard some of the other parents discussing how they couldn't believe that he still has meltdowns like this at his age. One of the kids who overheard the adults as well said, "Noah has autism. That's how he reacts sometimes." This was such a turning point for me to see how the other kids understood him. The parents, on the other hand, looked like deer caught in the headlights. This experience can teach us all a very powerful lesson: Just be kind. Have patience with others. We have no idea what other people are going through.

Before Noah came to our family, I thought I knew what patience was. After all, I was already the mother of three kids. I also thought I knew what unconditional love was. But my patience and ability to love has increased so much more by opening up my heart to this sweet little boy. Learning how to be Noah's mom has taught me so many lessons.

Having him in our lives has taught us all a whole different level of patience, understanding, and love. Every child is different, and each one has needs that are unique to them.

Noah really did turn our world upside down. He is an amazing kid and we all know that he came to our family for a reason. Although the journey has not always been easy, this is exactly where he is supposed to be.

Noah was the first missing piece of our family, and we became more complete when we brought him home. Our next missing piece was waiting for us in Ethiopia.

*Chapter 2*

# WE ALL HAVE A JOURNEY

## OUR JOURNEY TO ETHIOPIA

Life with four kids was chaotic, but we still felt like we were capable of more. We had a seven-seater Suburban at the time, so we still had room for another body. We researched countries with programs that fit our family, and we fell in love with Ethiopia. Since we had already completed an adoption, we knew how the system worked. We knew that the majority of families who adopt want babies and toddlers because older children potentially carry emotional baggage. As a result, the older kids are often left behind. Knowing this, our family requested an older child.

Children are usually relinquished in Ethiopia because of devastating, tragic life events. There's very little medical care available there, and basic illnesses can be life-ending due to the minimal supply and limited access to medication. Because of the death of a parent or the inability for parents to care for the basic needs of their children, parents relinquish their rights in the hopes that their children will have a better life. The adoption process is complex and lengthy. It took us several months to complete the documents required to adopt. We then waited to be matched with a child.

I was sitting in a meeting when I received a call from our adoption agency letting me know we had received a referral. I walked outside to take the call. When I walked back in, I was crying. I remember saying, "We're having a boy." At that point, everyone had tears in their eyes.

Ari was four and a half years old when we adopted him and brought him home. My husband and I made the journey to Ethiopia with two of our daughters, Emma and Olivia. After a long flight that began at Dulles Airport, we landed in the capital city of Addis Ababa. As I stepped off the plane, I felt transported from my ordinary life into a picture of raw beauty and simplicity.

We were brought to the orphanage with several other families who were also adopting children from Ethiopia. Watching these parents meet their children for the first time brought back a rush of emotions. Even now, just thinking about it, my eyes well up with happy tears. The first time you meet your child is truly a point in time that can't be replicated, whether you're adopting or giving birth. There are really no words for the love that fills your heart.

One of the most beautiful moments I had in those first few hours in Ethiopia, before meeting my own son, was watching other parents meet their children for the first time. One of the couples that we traveled with had tried for years to have a biological child, but they were unable to conceive. I can only imagine the pain and sadness they had to experience before arriving at this moment. But here they were—halfway across the world—about to meet their son for the first time. They were nervous, excited, and completely overwhelmed. We pulled up to the orphanage, and through the gate, we could see the nannies cuddling the babies and running after the toddlers. This new mother spotted her son and couldn't wait to get out of the van.

I will never forget the emotion in her face the first time she held her baby close. Gentle tears streaked down her cheeks as she carefully cradled what would become the greatest joy of her life. Seeing her hug her child for the very first time was a cherished moment that I tucked away in my heart forever. It's a reminder to me of true love. Of what our hearts are capable of when we allow ourselves to be vulnerable.

Witnessing this woman's beautiful meeting with her child made me impatient to see my own son. The older children lived in a different part of the orphanage, separate from the babies, so I had to wait.

## MEETING OUR SON FOR THE FIRST TIME

When we finally went inside to meet Ari, he knew who we were immediately. The orphanage had asked us to send a photo album that they could share with Ari to help him try to understand exactly what was going to happen. We took it one step further, though. Not only did we send a photo album with pictures of everyone in our family, but we all recorded our voices too. I thought it was a brilliant idea at the time I sent it. I later learned that the nannies weren't as delighted. They viewed the book much like we would a talking Cookie Monster toy given by a thoughtful grandparent. Apparently, Ari never stopped pushing the button. And by the time we got there, the batteries had died down so much, we sounded like aliens.

As we entered the orphanage, Ari was busy eating his lunch. I cautiously approached him. He looked at me, gave me a shy smile, and offered me some of his food. This amazing child—who was completely malnourished—was totally willing to share the little food he had with me.

I sat down next to him. He took my hand in his and he wouldn't let go. That was all he needed—it was all *I* needed. At the time, he was recovering from the mumps. He had ringworm covering the majority of his scalp. He had scars all over the bottom of his feet because he had never owned a pair of shoes. His legs were bowed from rickets and his belly distended from malnutrition. He had been through way too much in his short life—things kids should never have to endure.

But when he spoke, he had the sweetest high-pitched voice that warmed our hearts. He was adorable, and we loved him at first sight.

Ari had been in the orphanage for six months. He was barely four years old when his birth father dropped him off at one of the orphanage's drop-off points, and never came back. Ari's birth mother had passed away the previous year, and there was no one to care for him. He grew up in a mud hut without electricity or running water. With five older siblings, there just wasn't enough food for everyone. Ari's father had to make a tough decision.

Since Ari was the youngest, his father felt that he had the best chance of being adopted. Without Ari to feed, there was more food for the rest of the family. Before he made his final decision, Ari's birth father was reassured that Ari would be both cared for and fed in the orphanage. This helped to ease some of his sadness.

Like every other child at that orphanage, Ari was just waiting for someone to come for him—someone to love him.

Every time I sat down, all the kids would climb on my lap. They would softly kiss my face and lace their fingers with mine. They yearned for attention. All they wanted was for someone to love them and care for them—that's all they ever wanted.

My heart was drawn to these children. With boney frames and bloated bellies from a lifetime of malnutrition and disease, they were a reminder of the harsh reality faced by the people. And yet reflected in the bright smiles of each of those little ones was the spirit of a people that would never be broken. A proud people who continue on in life's journey despite the hardships and despite the uncertainty.

I would have adopted all of them if I could have. The one thing that comforted me was that all of the children in this orphanage had already been matched with families. They were just waiting for legal documents so that their forever family could come and bring them home.

### GETTING USED TO EACH OTHER

We were in Ethiopia for eight days. And during that time, we stayed in a guesthouse next to the orphanage. The small building offered four or five bedrooms for visiting families. We had the option to stay at a nearby hotel, but we chose the guesthouse because we wanted to be immersed in Ari's daily routine.

Every morning, right before sunrise—before the light peaked up over the horizon—we would wake up to the sound of chanting from a nearby Islamic mosque. The day began with the call to prayer, and I was mesmerized by the beautiful melodies. Most mornings we would head to the rooftop of the guesthouse to watch the city wake up. The smells, sights, and sounds were unlike anything I had experienced before. From the rooftop we could see hundreds and hundreds of the rusted tin roofs that were a part of the impoverished landscape of the capital city. Each house represented the story of a person and their ability to be resilient—even in the most difficult of situations.

The Ethiopian people we met were truly remarkable. Full of hope, even when the obstacles they faced seemed insurmountable. Full of life, in a country riddled by famine and disease, a place where death was often present. And full of love and happiness, even though the majority of the people had so little. Never have I seen such beautiful examples of the human spirit before.

Every morning, I would bring Ari from the orphanage to spend the day with us. He was allowed to go back and forth between our room and the orphanage anytime, but until we met his birth family, he wasn't allowed to stay with us at night.

During our days together before our birth family meeting,

I gave Ari new clothes and shoes and other things I had brought for him. But at night, without any prompting from me, he would take everything off, give it back to me, and put on his undersized pink Crocs and frayed clothing. He knew that if he took the items we gave him back to the orphanage, he would never see them again. There were so many children who longed for these things in the orphanage, and Ari didn't want them taken from him. I imagine it was his way of making sure that he would still have these treasures when he came back to us the next morning.

## HELLO AND GOOD-BYE

Four days into our eight-day stay, we were scheduled to travel and meet Ari's birth family. Ari was upset that he had to remain at the orphanage, even though the nannies explained that we were not leaving him for good. I'm sure he questioned if we were going to actually come back. Ari was from the southern part of Ethiopia, the Sidama region, and spoke Sidamo. The majority of the nannies at the orphanage spoke Amharic, the official language of Ethiopia. The language barrier between Ari and his nannies made verbal communication very difficult. The vocabulary that Ari and I shared consisted of about fifteen words such as: "Mom," "stop," "okay," and "do you have to pee?" His word of choice was "Mom."

Because he was so upset that we were leaving, and it was

difficult to help him understand why, I gave him my watch as a tangible promise that I would be back soon. It was my way of helping him understand that we weren't leaving for good. This helped to calm him down, and we were able to begin our journey to meet his birth family.

## A NEW KIND OF JOURNEY

To reach Ari's family home, we drove for almost six hours over bumpy dirt roads. Rather than two-story homes, paved sidewalks, and manicured lawns, there were small mud huts, crafted from the very earth they were built on, and fences constructed from salvaged bits of wood and broken string. The people used what they had to create not only a shelter to live in, but a structure that was truly a thing of beauty. As we drove through the different villages, I could see the open fires and smell the burning wood where families cooked their daily meals.

When we pulled up to their mud hut, our interpreter said, "Look, they decorated the home for you. Typically they only decorate for weddings and celebrations, so this is really a special moment."

They had taken pieces of plants and put them around the frame of the entrance. There wasn't an actual door, but the space was draped with a beautiful assortment of native flora that someone had cut down and placed there with great care. They had so little, yet they did all they could to make this visit special. They put a great deal of effort into preparing for our arrival.

Their home was rustically beautiful—the walls were molded from a mixture of clay and straw, the roof was thatched from palm fronds, and the floor was the original dirt the house was built on. The water was brought in from the river with buckets, as the closest well was two miles away. And no—they didn't have electricity. When we entered their hut, my eyes had to adjust to the dark space, lit only by sunlight that passed through the open entrance and small holes in the mud walls covered with a scrap of cloth that served as windows. The room was bare except for a couple of logs they brought for us to sit on. A smaller room off the main room held their only piece of furniture—one bed where Ari's father and five older siblings slept.

At first, it was hard to determine who was part of Ari's family. People from the village peered through the "windows" of the hut to get a small peek at us—the *ferengi*, aka "the foreigners." It seemed as if the whole village wanted to meet us. But with the interpreter's help, we were finally able to determine who the siblings were and to talk with them about Ari.

There were some pictures that had been sketched by one of Ari's sisters, who was probably fifteen years old. The drawings were obviously recreations of something that she may have seen in a book. She seemed incredibly intelligent. I imagine, like all of Ari's siblings, she wanted to be educated. My heart ached for them because I knew those opportunities were few and far between. The chances of getting an education in the circumstances in which they existed were minimal, and for a girl, those opportunities were almost nonexistent. Her responsibilities at home took precedence over her education.

We sat down and, through an interpreter, began a dialogue about Ari. We asked questions about the life he had there, and his father asked questions about our family. As we sat there, Olivia began kicking her foot back and forth, digging a rut in the ground. I looked at her and whispered, "Please stop making a hole in their floor, Olivia. This is their home. This is where they eat, sleep, and live." Her eyes grew big as she looked at me in shock. This was a life-changing journey for all of us.

## A DIFFICULT CONVERSATION

One of Ari's brothers started crying while we were talking. He seemed just slightly older than Ari.

"Is he crying because he's missing his brother?" I asked.

"No," the interpreter said, "he's crying because he wants to go with you too."

My heart broke. This was perhaps the hardest thing about our visit. What do you say? How do you tell a child that you're adopting his brother, but he has to stay? Obviously, adoption doesn't work that way. You don't just walk into someone's house and agree to adopt their child. Although we were elated to have Ari as part of our family, there was something very sad about the fact that Ari already had a family—a family that didn't have the resources to care for him.

The second hardest part of our visit was when Ari's birth father thanked us for adopting Ari. He actually thanked us. I had no idea how to respond to his gratitude. I knew that Ari's birth father made the decision to relinquish Ari because he had to—he had no other choice because they were starving. The only response I could think of was to promise that we would love him, care for him, and raise him to be proud of who he is and where he's from.

After being his mother now for over a decade, I can tell you that he was meant to be our son. He's happy and he is where he needs to be.

Before we left Ari's birth family, we made sure to take pictures of his home, his father, and his siblings so that I could create a photobook for Ari to keep. I felt it was so important that he had those memories of where he came from. They were his family first, and I will always be grateful to them because they shared Ari with us. I don't ever want my kids to feel like we erased any part of their life. I believe the more people who love you, the better off you are. I hope that one day Ari chooses to visit and see this important part of his life. Meeting his family gave us a greater understanding of his life and his journey, and a better understanding of ourselves.

## A NEW PERSPECTIVE

On our drive back to the orphanage, after Olivia finished hanging her head out the window and puking due to serial car sickness, we had an important discussion with our girls who, if I'm being honest, had never been exposed to poverty before—let alone developing-world poverty. Seeing our daughters' reactions to the experiences we had while in Ethiopia put things into perspective. I realized that we didn't spend enough time discussing diversity, and we didn't do a good job exposing them to the world. But there was no time like the present.

Most of our discussion revolved around trying to answer Olivia's questions of "Where do they go to the bathroom?" and "What do you mean they don't have toilet paper?" And Emma's questions of "How do they all fit in one bed?" and "Mom, could you cook a meal like that over an open fire? Actually, never mind on that one; you couldn't even cook a meal like that in a gourmet kitchen. No offense."

From the mouths of babes and through the eyes of a child!

"Girls," I said, "every single person in the world lives differently." It was a great lesson on just how diverse the world really is.

By the time we reached the orphanage, Olivia and Emma had run out of questions and were good to go. After three sets of clothing as a result of Olivia's car sickness, and a barrage of never-ending questions and comments, I was glad to get out of the car myself. That night, Ari was sleeping in our room, and it was as if he had always been a part of our family, except for the language barrier, which we were slowly learning to overcome.

Rob and I spent our time with Ari, and our girls spent the remainder of the trip in the infant rooms, holding the babies for hours on end. When it was time to go home, they were devastated. They wanted to take the babies with them. It was heartbreaking to watch them cry over leaving these children behind. As we departed the orphanage, we knew we would be back to adopt from Ethiopia again.

On our flight home, Ari did so well. There was a time when he started crying about something, but he didn't make any sound. He only had tears. This is how he always cried—tears, but no sound. Later, when he was older, he explained that they weren't allowed to cry at home. His birth father would not allow it, so he had learned to grieve in silence.

When our plane landed, I went to the restroom with the girls while Rob stayed with Ari. When we emerged from the bathroom, we found Ari and Rob examining the drinking fountain. Examining meant pushing the button upwards of a thousand times. Ari's shirt was soaked, and Rob had the biggest smile on his face. I had never seen a kid so excited about a drinking fountain in my life. And it made my heart smile to see the joy and love in Rob's eyes as he watched our son experience things for the first time.

To Ari, it must have been magical to see water flowing with the push of a button. Where he was from, in order to get water, they would have to walk to the river with a bucket and then carry it home. That fountain represented a whole new world to him.

He stood there pushing the button, saying, "Mom, mom, mom, mom, mom," over and over again. It was one of the only words he knew and understood.

"Yep, it's water," I said.

"What's he so excited about?" Olivia asked.

"Think about it," I said. "He has never seen things like this before. Just wait until we get home and he sees the light switch."

My hunch was correct. Electricity was even more fascinating to him. Thousands of times a day he would turn the lights on and then turn them back off again, all the time saying my name, over and over again, wanting me to share in the magic.

Ari's trip to America may have changed his life, but it was our journey to Ethiopia to bring him home that changed us even more. Adoption is an important part of our story—and our journey.

## YOUR STORY IS UNIQUE

We all have a story to tell. It's up to us to discover it. Our journey isn't just one thing—it comes to us in pieces. And each piece is part of our story.

When I share our story of adoption, people will often say to me, "Wow! Your story is amazing!" It took me a long time to realize that my story really can inspire people. But I believe that we all have inspiring stories to share. And we need to be more willing to share those stories.

One of my favorite things to do when I sit by a person is to say, "Tell me about yourself." Because it doesn't matter who I sit next to—I learn something from them. Sometimes I learn what not to do, but no matter what the lesson is, I learn something, and it's always worth the conversation. It's an important lesson that I'm constantly telling my kids: "You can always learn something from everyone you meet."

When you sit down and truly talk to someone, and really listen to them, you can learn remarkable things about them and their journey. Everyone's story is unique and different, and for most people, their story isn't finished yet.

Some of my best conversations happen within the confines of the cabin of an airplane. Once I sat next to a woman on a plane who had been married for over fifty years. Her husband was from India. They were married without the approval of either of their families, at a time when arranged marriage should have been the only option for him. But he met this beautiful girl from Iowa, fell in love, and couldn't imagine his life any other way. As I sat there mesmerized by her story, I was overwhelmed with gratitude for the opportunity I had to sit next to her and listen to her experience. We realized at the end of the flight that she had actually sat in the wrong seat. She was supposed to sit in the row in front of me. This experience was a reminder to always reach outside of our comfort zone and talk to people. You never know who you're going to meet. You can learn so much from just saying, "Hi, how are you?"

It's fascinating to me that the people who feel they're the most ordinary have the most incredible stories. Where they've grown up, how they've lived their lives, the experiences they've gone through—they're all unique and incredibly inspiring. Yet they don't see it in themselves.

I love asking people to share their stories with me. My kids laugh at me every time I talk to another stranger, but I think it's so important that I do it. I believe that the moment someone takes interest in another person's story, and truly listens to what they have to say, it makes that person's story even more powerful the next time they share it. By listening to the stories of others, we're helping them recognize that they do have a story to tell.

We're helping them discover their unique journey.

So many times, we focus on the destination, and we forget the value of the actual journey. We may get too caught up in finishing things. We may mistakenly believe that things need to be a certain way, and we're disappointed when life turns out differently. Often, our idea of what our journey should look like comes from comparisons we make with others who seem to have the perfect journey in life.

It's important for us to remember that our journey is ours.

My journey is mine, and I am living it the only way I know how—my way, because I only know how to be me.

You be you—and don't worry about how other people are doing it. And allow them to be who they're meant to be too.

When I was young, I constantly heard the phrase, "What would other people think?" But as an adult, I realized that I don't need to worry about what other people think. If I'm living my best life, and trying to be a good person, then why should I worry? The truth is, we shouldn't. Your life and your journey is going to be different than anyone else's. That's how it should be. That's what makes life beautiful— we're all uniquely different.

When we get caught up in what everybody else is doing, or what everybody else is thinking, we stop living our own life. And when we're living like someone else, we're not living authentically. We need to learn to own our own story and to be proud of the journey we're on. Own who you are, bumps in the road and all. They're all a part of you and your personal journey.

## YOUR EXTRAORDINARY JOURNEY MATTERS

Your journey may seem ordinary to you, but to someone

else, the small steps you take each day can be inspiring, motivational, and life-changing for them.

I think of all the mothers in the world who consider themselves ordinary. Many of these remarkable women see their journey as something expected and completely undervalued. But a good friend of mine sees the daily grind of child-rearing through a unique lens. She said that when her kids were young and the days were tough, she would always tell herself that she was tending her garden. There's never been a truer statement.

To the children who they care for, each mother's actions are a cherished reminder that they are loved. Mothers have one of the most important jobs in the world. We are helping to raise the next generation of humans, and it's our responsibility to teach these small humans kindness, patience, and respect for others. For me, being a mother is one of the biggest parts of my journey.

I often laugh when I see the calculations of the salary that a stay-at-home mom should be receiving. If she actually got paid for all of the different jobs that she does on a daily basis, it would be equivalent to the CEO of a major corporation. (I'm still waiting for my check in the mail that covers all the back-pay from being the CEO of the Knego corporation.)

Seriously, though, mothers are worth so much! But sometimes I think moms are so busy that they forget to take a step back and realize how important their job really is. Because cooking and cleaning and grocery shopping and changing diapers and shuttling children around and helping to read and teaching decimals and folding laundry and any number of other things are the things moms (and even dads) do every day, they fail to see the splendor in it. On top of that, there are so many women who do all the mom things and work another job or two as well. Moms are miracle workers, but they rarely see that in themselves.

## YOU'RE SO MUCH MORE THAN A JOB TITLE

I firmly believe that no matter what you do, whether you're a stay-at-home mom, or you're a working mom, or an adoptive mom, or a foster mom, or you're not a mom at all and your job title is something completely different—your journey matters. You matter, and you make a difference.

I loved reading a volunteer application where a woman wrote "household engineer" as her job title. What a great way to describe what she does. She was proud of her life. This is exactly how we should feel no matter what our job is. It's not about the job we do; it's about how we do that job and the kind of person we are.

Imagine what kind of an impact a physician with a "god

complex" can have, compared to a physician who's simply a good human being, just trying to do their best in the world. I look at my husband, Rob, and he does amazing things every day. He really does. He saves people all the time. That's what he does. But he is a really good human, and he doesn't define himself by the fact that he has "Doctor" in front of his name. He defines himself by how he treats other people.

Some people have the luxury of getting a college education, and some people don't because the finances just aren't there. But education doesn't change who a person is as a human. It's the same with fame and money. These things don't add more value to a person as a human being. If you're a good human, you're a good human, regardless of what you do or have.

### OWN WHO YOU ARE AND CELEBRATE IT

We may never know the impact we have—doing those small and simple things each day—but they will always have an impact and touch people's lives for good.

For the mother struggling with a new baby, your offer to take her older child to preschool may not seem like a huge thing to you; but to that struggling mother, it's an enormous act of kindness that eases and brightens her day. Smiling at someone on the train ride home may not seem like a big deal to you; but to the person you smile at, it may lift them from thoughts of sadness and despair.

I'll never forget one day when I was in the Starbucks drive-through. When I got to the window to pay for my order, instead of asking for payment, the employee handed me a little card that simply said, "Pay it forward." The person ahead of me had paid for my coffee and given me an invitation to do the same for someone else. It was such a tiny gesture in the overall scheme of things. It cost them three bucks, but it made my day. It may seem ridiculous, but that small act meant so much to me. I really did have a great day, and I will never forget it. The next time I went through the drive-through, I paid it forward.

When you choose to be the good in the world, it's not just someone else's life you're changing; it's your own. You start to see the world differently, and it feels fantastic! Your act of good might seem like it's simple or basic, but it could be something that the person will remember forever, like the Starbuck's cup of coffee. Even now when I think about it, it inspires me. Your kind acts could do that for someone else.

I think we often go through our lives feeling like we're so busy that we can't possibly make a difference. We're never too busy to do something good. Smile at someone in the grocery store, hold the door open for a coworker, send a kind text to a friend you haven't seen in a while, invite your neighbors over for dinner. Make a difference.

When you're doing good, you always get back more than you give.

## OPEN YOURSELF UP TO NEW POSSIBILITIES

Not only do we need to recognize that we're already doing good in our everyday actions, but we need to open ourselves up to all of the possibilities around us. When we close ourselves off, we miss those opportunities. There's always more good we can do—so many ways that we can step up, do a little more, and be a little better. Once you realize what you're capable of, there's no limit to the good you can do for others. I had no idea what my life could be until I opened myself up to new possibilities and realized what I was capable of.

They say the journey of a thousand miles starts with a single step, but I would say the journey begins with the choice to take that step. The path that lies ahead depends on the choice that started it.

*Chapter 3*

# THE POWER OF CHOICE

## A UNANIMOUS DECISION

When Rob and I decided that we wanted to adopt, we didn't make the decision without first discussing it with the whole family. We wanted our kids to be in on the process because it wasn't just Rob and me who would have to step up—we would all have to contribute to the adjustment of our new child. Adoption is a huge decision that affects everyone in the family.

When we adopted Noah, the kids were younger, and I'm sure they all said yes just because it seemed like a really cool thing to them to have a new brother. The second time, when we made the decision to adopt Ari, we put it to a vote, and everyone said yes again.

Each time we brought another child into our home, the adjustments required of the children we already had were even greater. The kids had to be all in, because that's how it works in a big family. The more children you have, the more everyone has to be willing to compromise and share because we only have so much time and resources to give. But we always have more than enough love.

The third time around, we had five kids already, and family life was chaotic. There was never a dull moment. Noah was especially tough because of his sensory challenges, which would cause him to cry and scream a lot of the time. Some daily hurdles included teeth brushing, maintaining an adequate diet for a toddler, and riding in the car. These things might seem basic, but for a child with sensory issues, these tasks can sometimes be completely overwhelming. At the time, adding a sixth child into the mix seemed crazy. But what is life without a little bit of crazy?

Rob and I agreed that the decision to adopt had to be unanimous, because it really does take a village to raise a child. And when you already have a village—seven people in a family, and you want to bump it up to eight—the existing seven better all be on board.

A year after returning from Ethiopia with Ari, we wanted to see what the family really thought about adopting again.

We sat all of our kids down around the table and had a family council.

"I know when we left Ethiopia with Ari, we said we'd go back to adopt again," I said, "but we really want to know what you guys think about it now. Dad and I have talked about it, and we would like to start the process."

Of course, the girls jumped on it and named several of the children they had met in the orphanage on our trip to adopt Ari and asked if we could adopt them.

"Guys, we have talked about this," I said. "Those kids already had families coming for them. They aren't in the orphanage anymore. They've all been adopted. We'd like to apply to adopt an older boy again, but we want to see what you guys think about it."

We gave everyone a piece of paper and a pen, and we sat there watching them as they thought about it and then wrote their answer. As I watched Jacob, I could only imagine what he might have been thinking. Maybe something like, "How many more kids will I need to share my Xbox with?" He was the oldest, and he had already given so much for the others. Olivia was the first to write her response. She didn't even have to think about it, which amazed me. She was six, but she was a determined six.

After everyone wrote down their responses, we read them aloud. As a mom, I can't even begin to explain the love I felt in my heart for each of these little humans. Every time I read a "yes" vote, I couldn't help but think of how lucky I am to be their mom. Olivia's reaction was particularly touching to me.

"Olivia," I said, "you didn't even hesitate when you wrote down your answer."

"Mom," she said with confidence, "we're talking about the life of another child. How could anyone vote no?"

That was such a huge statement from someone so small.

The kids understood that we would all have to devote countless hours to the adjustment of their new sibling—hours that would no longer be devoted to them. Yet each answer was a simple yes. It was unanimous. We would adopt again. Each of us had to make a choice, but the result of that unanimous decision has been life-changing for all of us.

## LIFE IS ABOUT CHOICES

Every day, we're faced with choices—choices that can change the journey of our life and the lives of those we know and love. We can choose to move forward, or we can bury our head in the sand and put on blinders to the world around us.

Sometimes the blinders that we choose to wear are our own negative self-talk. We talk ourselves out of doing something good before we ever get the opportunity to do it. We don't vote, because we don't think it will matter. We don't stand up for something, because we don't feel like anyone will even listen. We can go our whole lives never speaking up because we are afraid that what we have to say won't even matter.

But people do care. The world cares. Somebody is always willing to listen. It's important to choose to use your voice and stand up for what you believe in. Things might not change instantaneously, but if nobody ever stood up for the things they believed in, think about how different our history would be. Every moment in time that changed the future of our world began because of the one person who stood up and used their voice—women's rights, the abolishment of slavery, desegregation. Change began with one person choosing to stand up for what they believed in and what was right for humanity.

If we continue to live our lives in a world we believe we can never change, we start to become indifferent to that world. Rather than spark change, we find ourselves complaining, "Well, I don't like how things are, but there's nothing I can do about it." When we think this way, we start to believe that our voice doesn't matter. But our voice does matter.

When Rosa Parks refused to get up from her seat on the

bus, an entire group of people began to stand up for their rights as humans. She probably had no idea that her choice would bring about such significant social change. But rather than complain about the discrimination she faced on a daily basis, Rosa Parks decided to do something about it. She did what she felt was right, not what was easy. She became a catalyst for good herself, because a different world can't be built by indifferent people.

## WHAT WILL YOU CHOOSE?

It has been my experience that we, as human beings, tend to spend a lot of our time complaining about things rather than stepping up to fix them. I'm sure all of us, at some point, have complained about a problem, but were unwilling to make a change, or to volunteer to help fix it. I'm totally guilty of this. But change begins with us—and the choices that we make. We can be a part of the problem, or we can be a part of the solution.

We all have the opportunity to help create positive change, but we often find ourselves thinking, "I'm already really busy, and how much of a difference can I really make?" This is especially true when we're talking about addressing massive social problems, like tackling world hunger or finding a cure for cancer. But it pops up all the time in our everyday lives as well. When I catch myself thinking this way, it helps to really think about the little changes that happen every day because I am choosing to act. We may not be able to change the entire world, but we can change a small part of it for someone. You can take food to the local food pantry, volunteer at an assisted living center, or help a neighbor in need. Your small contributions can make a big difference. Someone's life will be impacted for the better because you chose to step up, in even just a little way.

Often we put off doing good, because our efforts feel too small and unimpactful. But an experience I had with Jacob helped me understand the impact of simple actions. In 2007, Rob, Jacob, and I traveled on a medical mission to Ghana. Jacob was eleven. He knew we were going to visit a school on the trip and decided that he wanted to collect school supplies and raise funds for the school. He put together a flyer and gave it to his classmates and his teachers. The teachers shared it with the entire school.

When we arrived at the airport to check our bags for the flight, we had ten duffel bags full of school supplies, clothes, soccer balls, toothbrushes, and first-aid kits. When the airline agent found out what was in the duffel bags, she didn't charge anything for the extra bags. In addition to the supplies, Jacob had also raised $2,000 in cash from kids, their parents, and our friends—generous people wanting to help. With the $2,000 that Jacob raised, we were able to purchase mosquito nets to protect the students from malaria, mattresses to take the place of the wooden boards that some of the kids slept on, and enough rice to last for months.

The look on the faces of the children and the teachers at the school in Ghana was something that we will never forget. One pencil, one pad of paper, one dollar, added up to a life-changing experience.

So many times, when it comes to donations, people are hesitant to give because they feel that they have to give a significant amount for it to matter. Giving a dollar makes a difference. Giving a pencil makes a difference. Enlisting other people to give a dollar makes a whole lot of difference. The ripple effect of giving can make a massive difference. If one child, like Jacob, can make such a huge difference in a community, imagine what we as adults can do if we actually make the choice to do something.

**CHOOSE TO STEP OUT OF LINE**

We can choose to be happy, or we can choose to be miserable. We can also choose to stand up and say something, or we can choose to do nothing. But the world isn't going to change if we just sit back and do nothing. In other words, if everybody sat back and did nothing, nothing would ever change.

Choosing to step up is never easy. As a matter of fact,

there are very few things in life that are going to be easy. But if it's the right thing to do, then the choice is always worth it.

Alex Borstein, a Jewish actress, who in 2019 won an Emmy for best supporting actress in a comedy, gave an incredibly powerful acceptance speech about her grandmother who was a Holocaust survivor. She was in line at a camp, about to be shot and pushed into a pit. She asked the guard, "What happens if I step out of line?"

The guard said he didn't have the heart to shoot her, but someone else would. She stepped out of line anyway. She escaped and survived. The only reason she survived is because she chose to step out of line. That may have been one of the most difficult decisions she ever had to make, but it's a choice that saved her life. That choice changed her world, her children's world, and the world of her grandchildren—not to mention the world of TV and film. When possible, we need to choose to step out of line. The choices we make often have a much larger impact than we even realize.

## BE THE CHANGE

Change is rarely grand and glorious. More often than not, it begins with changing the way you see yourself and the way you approach things.

Oftentimes, the change the world needs is our own change of heart.

Being more open-minded allows the change to start with you, and that's a great place to start. Just because you've done something the same way for years doesn't mean that there's not another way of doing it. Be open to learning something new and to learning from other people. Let me give you a small example from my own life.

I'm not a kumbaya kind of person. My kids will tell you that they've probably seen me cry only a handful of times. It's not that I associate tears with weakness—it's actually quite the opposite. I wish I was able to cry more because I think there's something extremely therapeutic in letting your true emotions flow by allowing yourself to be vulnerable and just being you.

Sometimes I questioned why I didn't cry over things that seemed tear-worthy. I was like Cameron Diaz in the movie *The Holiday*, unable to force a tear—except I'm not really her. After constantly hearing how tough I was for forty years, it's just what I became. I put up a barrier, holding in my emotions, becoming what everyone else believed me to be.

One day, that all changed. There I was, sitting in a room surrounded by six hundred women, crying my eyes out over the Colbie Caillat video, *Try*.

Why? At that moment I realized everything I had been harboring over the years. Feelings of doubt, fear, and not being enough. Sitting there in that moment, listening to other women speak about their struggles, I realized that I was not alone. Sharing my stories allowed me to truly be me. I am tough. I am sensitive. I am beautiful. I am me.

Comparison can be the thief of happiness. Why do we do this to ourselves? Why do we compare ourselves to others? Why do we struggle to just be who we are? Why can't we just support other women without judgment, comparison, or jealousy? Be UnOrdinary. Be kind. Be *you*.

"Don't judge someone until you've walked a mile in their shoes." I've heard this my whole life. But the reality is that you can never walk in someone else's shoes. You'll never be in the exact same situation as anyone else, which means you should never judge anyone else.

When we're faced with choices like these that define us, we can choose to be helpful, or we can choose to be hurtful. In a world where you can be anything, be kind. And let change begin with you.

## SMALL CHOICES OFTEN LEAD TO GREATER GOOD

Every day, we have opportunities that come our way—

opportunities that, if we choose to accept, can lead to even greater good in our lives.

In 2011, our friends were leading a Young Leadership mission to Israel. I really wanted to support them and asked Rob if he'd be willing to go with me.

Rob grew up Catholic, but more agnostic than anything. We had been married for twenty years, and although we weren't religious, the customs and values of Judaism were very important to our family. We were raising the kids Jewish. And even though Rob wasn't Jewish, he went with me to synagogue on the High Holidays and totally supported having a Jewish family.

His answer to my question about the trip was, "I don't know, Simone. I'm not Jewish. Everybody who's going on this trip is Jewish. I don't want to feel like an outsider, and I don't want to feel uncomfortable."

"Nobody's going to make you feel that way," I said. "Our friends are leading it, and we should go and support them." A lengthy conversation ensued, and the decision was finally made.

He reluctantly agreed but said, "I'm not going to tell anybody I'm not Jewish."

"You do you," I said. "You don't have to change how you do things for anybody else. We're going to have a great time."

We had an amazing time. We met so many interesting people and made friendships with individuals and couples that we would have never met in any other realm. People we are still in contact with today. Rob was relaxed and totally comfortable the entire trip. For the first time, Rob really felt like he was part of a community.

## CHOOSING TO CHANGE

At the end of the mission, we sat down in a small room with our caucus, the forty other people on our bus. These were people we had really come to know and respect. Together, we talked about the most impactful moments of the trip for each of us. Rob hadn't told me all that he had been feeling up to this point. When he started talking, I just sat in awe.

He told everyone he wasn't Jewish. He shared how he was embarrassed to tell people this at the beginning of our trip. He explained how this mission changed his outlook on religion and community. And then, with tears in his eyes, he said that upon returning home, he would start his conversion process.

I had no idea this was what he was thinking or that this trip would be so life-changing for our family. In our twenty years of marriage, I never thought he would convert to Judaism. It was never even a discussion. He knew he didn't have to do it for me, because I loved him exactly as he was. But there we were, in a roomful of friends who were strangers just days before, and Rob was saying he was going to convert to Judaism. The most powerful piece for me was that it was all his choice. That made his conversion much deeper and much more personal for both of us.

In Judaism, typically at the age of thirteen, young adults go through a coming-of-age ritual. Girls have a bat mitzvah while boys have a bar mitzvah. But this ritual isn't just about coming-of-age; it's about taking responsibility for your actions and realizing that you are now a full-fledged member of the Jewish community. Rob studied for a year with our rabbi and completed his conversion in 2012, two weeks before Emma's bat mitzvah. Although Rob was a bit older than the typical bar mitzvah boy, he had his bar mitzvah at Emma's bat mitzvah. It was an emotional experience for our family to see Rob move through the process. Several friends from our trip attended. There wasn't a dry eye in the synagogue.

It was such a special event in our life, and that choice completed our Jewish family. But it's really more than that. We are the models for our children. When our children saw that Rob made that choice—not because I told him to or asked him to, but because he really felt like he was part of something greater—it made a lasting impact on our kids. It taught them that we should always be open to change. Here Rob was, fifty years old, and he had made a choice that would impact our family for the rest of our lives.

When Rob and I made the choice to support our friends and join them on their trip to Israel, neither one of us knew the impact that single choice would make in the direction of our lives. Looking back, I am so grateful for the journey and the choice that was made that got us here.

There are going to be times in your life where you are faced with a decision, and as I said before, you can put your head in the sand and stay right where you are, or you can choose to do something, to go somewhere, to help someone, and it may just change your life. And oftentimes, the things we hesitate to do just might be the exact things we need to do.

In a million years, Rob never thought that he would love visiting and studying with a rabbi, but those were some of his favorite times. They would talk for hours not just about religion, but about philosophy and life in general. It really opened up his eyes to the world and the diversity in it. Rob taught all of us that it is good to make changes in your life, no matter what your age, and to always be open to a new way of seeing things.

## SEEING THE WORLD IN A NEW LIGHT

When the light in a room is turned on, everything looks different. By opening our eyes to a new way of seeing things, the world will look different too. Rob experienced this with Judaism, and our children experienced it with traveling to Ethiopia. Olivia's willingness to adopt again came because we had already adopted twice. She had visited Ethiopia, and she had seen and interacted with the amazing children at the orphanage. She knew how they lived and how desperately they wanted someone to love them.

It was as if the light was turned on and her eyes were opened to a new way of seeing the world. Because of this, her answer to our adoption question was, without any hesitation, a loud "YES"! She understood. She had already made the choice before our question was even asked, because the experiences she already had helped her to see the world differently. Every experience we have and every choice we make gives us a little more light by which we can see the world just a little more clearly.

*Chapter 4*

# ONE LIFE TO LIVE

## A JOURNEY TO THE HEART

Finding fulfillment in life is what I believe brings the greatest joy. How we find fulfillment will be different for each of us. We all have our own journey to walk and our own timeline to keep. My fulfillment looks different than yours, and as I said before, no two journeys are the same.

One of the greatest chapters of our journey was adoption, and fulfillment for our family meant filling the minivan. We traded in the Suburban after we brought Ari home, and we bought an eight-passenger minivan. We again had room for one more. Our adoptions of Noah, Ari, and Mili as our caboose were each so different. But through them, we were able to add the missing pieces to our family and finally fill our minivan.

Of all their adoption stories, Mili's was the most eye-opening, not only because of the journey we took to reach her birth family, but because of the journey we took to reach her heart. After we adopted Ari, we knew that we still wanted to adopt one more time. So about a year after we brought him home, we decided to go all in and apply for one last adoption in Ethiopia.

We applied once again for an older boy, but we were completely surprised when we found out we were having a two-year-old little girl. We saw Mili for the first time in a picture. There she was, standing all alone in a light pink dress that was obviously a community outfit covering the shirt and black pants that could be seen poking out from underneath it. It made me wonder how many other little girls were wearing the same pink dress in their referral picture—probably too many to count.

In addition to the oversized dress, Mili was wearing shoes that were obviously way too big for her, and she looked scared beyond words. Her eyes told such a tragic story of loss. I had never before seen eyes that sad. Her head was shaven, and she wore a sign around her neck with her last name written on it in the most beautiful handwriting. My heart broke and instantly we knew our decision to adopt one more time was absolutely the right decision. No one, especially a child, should ever be that sad. And although we couldn't relieve everyone's suffering—we could help to relieve hers.

When it came time to bring Mili home, Rob stayed back with the other kids, and Jacob and I flew to Ethiopia. When we first met Mili, she was so scared that just getting close to her caused her anxiety. And if we tried to pick her up, her whole body would go limp and she would pass out in our arms.

At the orphanage, Mili lived in a room lined with cribs with several other babies and toddlers. At the time, there was a measles outbreak, so the babies and toddlers were confined to their room and spent most of their day in their cribs. Jacob and I spent our days sitting next to Mili's crib, trying to get her used to us. Rather than picking her up and holding her, we would interact with her through the rails of the crib so that she didn't feel threatened.

She was by far the sickest of our kids when we adopted her. She had kwashiorkor, a protein deficiency that, among other symptoms, caused her to have an extremely distended abdomen. She couldn't sit up and could barely walk. She had giardia from unclean water, and she had patches of hair missing from her head due to a severe case of ringworm. She was missing a toenail, a fingernail, and had a fire burn on her belly. Her nose was continually running, and when she spoke, she had a raspy voice. She sounded like a chain smoker because of the constant crud in her lungs. And—she was absolutely gorgeous.

Mili was meant to be my child, I knew that, yet my presence

completely stressed her out. Here I was, trying as hard as I could to help her feel safe and secure. And there she was, fragile and suffering. I felt sad. I felt angry. And I felt a bit helpless. But this wasn't about me. It was about her and what she had been through. I just wanted to pick her up and hug her and tell her that everything was going to be okay, but the adoption journey isn't like that. Many of the kids in orphanages have experienced hard things—things that no one should have to experience. And because of this, it takes time, patience, and a lot of love to help them feel safe again. And even then, sometimes the struggles don't go away. All we could do was wait for Mili to trust us.

A few days passed, and although Mili seemed to have become accustomed to our presence, she was still so scared. At times I questioned myself, my abilities, and my thought process. Was I making the right choice for her? Was I truly thinking about what was best for her? My answer always came back as, "Yes!"

I think a lot of times people see adoption as a fairy tale—a perfect story with a magical ending. Adoption is hard. These are kids who have lost everything they once knew, everything they had. They didn't choose this life—but we did. And it was our job to figure out how to make this little girl realize that we were her forever family.

I brought a miniature soccer ball for her to play with. I

would throw the ball to her and, eventually, she would throw it back to me out of the crib. This game was really what started to open her up and allowed us to get closer to her. She would finally let me touch her—just a little—and then she would run to the other side of the crib. It became a game. Still, I kept thinking to myself, "Okay, how am I going to get this girl home?"

On the fifth day of us being there, Mili let me feed her. I wasn't expecting it, but it was such a relief to me. I walked into the room and the nanny seemed a bit overwhelmed. All the kids wanted their breakfast, and since it was such a small space, it was difficult to maneuver from kid to kid. I actually thought she would ask me to feed one of the other kids, but she pointed me to Mili. I laughed a little as I thought to myself, "Yeah, right."

I don't know if it was because she was just hungry or because something changed. Maybe I was wearing her favorite color. All I know is that as I moved the spoon of porridge toward her, she opened her mouth—and she ate the entire bowl. My heart leaped with joy. I thought to myself, "Okay, I can get her home now. If I can feed her, I can get her home."

That was the turning point in our relationship. I gained the confidence that I needed to flourish as Mili's mom, and she finally knew that she would be safe with me. It took small and simple steps. It took time, patience, and above all, love.

But all those little things brought about a complete change of heart.

## BEYOND NOWHERE

A fulfilling life is not complete without a little adventure sprinkled throughout. It's what keeps things interesting and keeps us wanting to come back for more.

Just like when we adopted Ari, we made a trip to visit with Mili's birth family. This was an adventure in the truest sense of the word. After riding for what seemed like forever through rough terrain, the vehicle stopped. We had gone as far as we could—the rest of the journey would have to be on foot. Several hours beyond the middle of nowhere, we were hiking in the hills of Southern Ethiopia, trying to find Mili's birth family, following the few inconsistent instructions the guide could get from the local people. We were wandering like nomads, except for the fact that we were extremely directionally challenged. We were being followed by about thirty random children, fascinated by our obvious lack of direction and our inability to speak their language. And to add to the excitement, night was falling fast.

Like Ari's birth family, Mili's family lived quite a distance away from the orphanage. But unlike the dusty, dry valleys of Ari's birthplace, the landscape here was one complete with gushing waterfalls, trickling streams, and lush, green vegetation. The rainy season was in full force and had transformed a barren plateau into a thriving, vibrant ecosystem. The surrounding hills were peppered with huts that were unlike anything I had ever seen before, artistically woven from grass and reeds and vastly different from the mud huts in Ari's village. It's difficult to imagine the time they must have invested in crafting these homes. Every hut was woven with such detail, like they were to be exhibited in a gallery, each one so uniquely beautiful. Everywhere I looked, I was surrounded by beauty.

There was no GPS, Google Maps, not even directional markers to get us to where we were going. We had to rely on good old-fashioned word of mouth. They lived in the hills, and the only way to find them was to have the guide ask directions from the other villagers. We made our way from hut to hut, looking for any clue that would lead us to the family. The hike was not easy, and no, we didn't have water. Who knew that we were going to hike? Not me. I honestly wondered if we would ever find them.

After what we felt like a full day of wandering—which we later found out was only two hours—we were greeted by a messenger from the village where Mili's birth family lived. Word had spread throughout the hills that there were lost white people aimlessly wandering the villages. Fortunately, they knew where we were supposed to be.

Though it wasn't what I had expected, it was an amazing experience. We met so many people that day. Everyone wanted me to take their picture and show them the image. We may not have had GPS, but we had a digital camera, which was way more important. The look on their faces as they saw their reflection in the camera screen is a memory that I will never forget. Pure joy.

We reached the family hut around 5:00 p.m. Through an interpreter, we were able to speak with her aunt, uncle, and two of her three siblings. We learned Mili's birthparents had passed away shortly after she was born, and the aunt and uncle were raising all of the kids. They weren't able to manage everything and reluctantly decided to relinquish Mili. We could tell it was a very tough decision for them as the aunt had a steady stream of tears running down her cheeks almost the entire time we were there—it was heart-breaking. They asked a lot of questions about our life and our other kids. Her uncle's face was beaming when he realized that Mili was going to be able to go to school.

While we were visiting, they offered us food and insisted that we eat with them. Mili's family lived in a rural area without electricity or running water. No electricity equals no refrigeration. Their diet consisted mainly of Kocho, a staple food derived from *enset*, which is also known as "false banana."

Enset, looks like a banana tree, but it doesn't produce bananas. They harvest the stalk of the plant, chop it up, wrap it in the leaves, and then bury it in the ground. About three months later, once it's fermented, they remove it from the ground, cut it, knead it, and remove all of the fibrous pieces. At this point it looks like sand, and tastes like...sand. Some people fry it into bread, but we ate it as it was. It almost looked like couscous—but it definitely didn't taste like couscous. I'm willing to try anything. I'm definitely not scared of food. I've eaten crickets and grasshoppers before—on purpose—so this was no big deal. They served the Kocho with warm, curdled milk. Definitely a meal to remember.

The Kocho, aka sand, is served in one communal container, and everyone eats from it with their hands. I watched as each person dipped their hand into the bowl, took a small portion of food, and licked their fingers. Whatever was left on their fingers, they would flick back into the bowl, and then it was the next person's turn. As I observed this scene and realized what I was going to be asked to do, I couldn't help thinking to myself, "If I don't catch something from this, it'll be a miracle. I'm eating food that was buried in the ground, fermented, and then communally shared with everybody's spit going back into the food they want me to eat." I respectfully ate the food they offered me, and thankfully I didn't get sick.

Enter economic privilege: As a side note, I live a life where I get to decide not only how many times I want to eat each day, but what I want to eat, who I want to eat with, and how much I want to eat. I'm not limited by what I can grow in my yard, what I can trade for, or unpredictable weather cycles. I've never gone to sleep with hunger pains. I've only lost weight because of a diet, not starvation. And I've never had to tell my kids that there will not be food on the table because we just don't have the resources to feed them. I'm fortunate and thankful every day for the gifts that I've been given and for those I'm able to share. And yes—there are also days that I take things for granted.

When the food got to Jacob, he was willing to try the food, but he whispered to me, "I can't drink the milk. There's just no way, Mom." The milk was also passed around in a communal container, and when it got to Jacob, he just couldn't stomach it.

I turned to the interpreter and asked, "Is it going to cause an international incident if he doesn't drink the milk?" I was such a wordsmith.

"No," our interpreter said, "I'll explain it to them."

I thought he was going to say something like, "Oh, he has a food allergy." But the interpreter said they had no idea what a food allergy was. Instead, he told the family that we don't drink our milk that way, that we drink it cold instead. The look on their faces was one of confusion. They were shocked, and it probably sounded as bad to them as their milk looked to us. After Jacob was relieved of milk-drinking duty, the giant mug was passed to me. I peered into the large vessel before I took a sip. I saw chunks of curdles floating on the top of the off-white liquid. It was actually a bit comical because I'm married to a man who will not even smell milk if it's beyond the expiration date, and here I was drinking it.

To be respectful, I took a sip of the milk, and sure enough, it tasted like sour milk. I did my best to drink it through my teeth to keep the chunks from flowing into my mouth. It was truly an educational experience.

My main goal was to do whatever I could to not be disrespectful. Although their customs were very different from what I was used to, it was interesting to learn about their lives. This family invited us into their home and were willing to share what little food they had with us. For them, that was a huge sacrifice.

Suddenly, the uncle jumped to his feet and shouted a few words to the adults outside of the hut. We were then offered the greatest gift ever. The interpreter's translation was as follows: They wanted to slaughter their goat, cook it over their fire pit, and then share it with us. It should take a maximum of about fifteen minutes to prepare—fifteen minutes to slaughter the goat and cook it to well done on the fire. I was a math major and this definitely did not add up.

To be honest, I had heard the goat mewing from the moment we sat down. I think he was asking me to leave quickly and not have the desire to put him into my belly. Since it was already late, I listened to the goat. In my mind, I'm sure he silently thanked me. Also, our interpreter assured us they wouldn't mind if we declined their offer because it meant more food for their family. Jacob and I both breathed a big sigh of relief.

We said our goodbyes, thanked them for their hospitality, and promised to love Mili with every ounce of our being. They walked with us to the place where we met our vehicle. We had obviously taken the long route on the way in. It only took us about fifteen minutes on the way out. As we began to drive away, I looked in the rearview mirror and saw Mili's aunt, tears streaming down her cheeks, holding her hand up in the air to wave goodbye. My heart hurt.

## LIFE PRICE

As we tried to leave, the children from the village surrounded the car. They were singing and chanting, and I had no clue what was happening. Our driver rolled down his window and began screaming at the kids. They wouldn't move. He got out of the car and tried to shoo them away.

They stepped back about two feet. It seemed like a game to them. When he got back into the car, they took a step toward the vehicle. The driver was now screaming at the top of his lungs for them to move back.

At first, I thought, "I get it...He wants to leave but they don't want us to." I could see why he was yelling. It was late and we needed to get home. But then the driver explained to me what the real issue was.

Very few people venture into these villages in Ethiopia. The kids aren't used to cars, so when they see one, they're fascinated by them. His concern was not so much about their safety, but what would happen to him if he were to hit one of the kids with the car. He explained to me that he would have to pay the "life price" if he were to kill one of the kids with his car.

I absolutely wasn't expecting this explanation. He explained that there was a dollar value placed on a life in Ethiopia. I'm not sure if it was just in the rural areas, but it was true of where we were at that moment. If he were to kill someone, even accidentally, he would have to pay a year's worth of his wages to their family. At the time, that was the equivalent of $500 US dollars. Just let that sink in.

And with that piece of newfound information, we slowly made our way back to civilization.

Meeting Mili's birth family was an experience that will forever be engrained in my heart and my mind.

It was an adventure I'll never forget and brought lessons that I'll always treasure. Life is precious, and each life has value that goes far beyond our "life price." Our challenge is to value the life we've been given and use that life to bring greater value to those around us.

## BE OPEN TO WHERE YOUR JOURNEY TAKES YOU

I have just one sibling—my sister, Michelle, who is a psychiatrist in Switzerland. Michelle met her husband, Thomas, while they were both studying at the University of Florida. They fell in love, married, and moved to his native Switzerland. My sister told me that she thought it would be a great adventure to move to Switzerland with Thomas, and she wasn't wrong.

Not only did she have to adjust to the cold temperature, but she had to learn how to cook with fresh ingredients without using prepackaged meals—they don't even have frozen waffles or Kraft Mac and Cheese where she lives—and she had to learn how to practice medicine in Swiss German. But because she was open to a new way of living, she moved beyond the struggle and embraced a greater life. Sometimes, that's what our journey will require of us.

Michelle became accustomed to the cold, although I don't know if she'll ever really love it. She even knows how to ski—a skill she picked up in her thirties. She learned how to make some amazingly delicious meals, and when it comes to the language, she's perfectly bilingual. It's pretty impressive to listen to her. She absolutely met the challenges she was faced with, and she came out better for it.

Never would I have thought that this is what her life would be. And I'm sure growing up, she never imagined she would be living in a small village in Switzerland, practicing psychiatry, in the cold and snow, cooking meals from scratch with Thomas and their two children, Sabrina and Benji. But she's really happy there.

Life is different everywhere you go. Respect it, learn from it, take it all in, and appreciate it. This is something I discovered while visiting my sister.

We decided to go see a Harry Potter movie at a local cinema. Because what could be better than Harry Potter in subtitles? In the middle of the movie, the lights turned on and the film stopped playing.

"What's happening?" I asked.

"Oh, it's intermission," she said like it was no big deal.

"Intermission?" I said. "In a movie?" I'm sure I sounded like someone who's never been out in the world before. But in my head I thought, "Hi, my name is Simone Knego and we don't have movie intermissions in the US, so it's unthinkable that you would have them here. We have to get things done—FAST, QUICK—so we can move on to the next thing. If we had an intermission in a Harry Potter movie, people just might riot."

"Yeah," she said. "We have fifteen minutes to go out and get a drink, get some coffee, or get a snack."

*Hmmm. Very interesting.*

That's just how it worked there. And you know what? I kind of liked it. Actually, it was brilliant! Finally, a movie where I didn't have to miss even one scene, because I could use the restroom during the intermission. Thank you, Switzerland.

I always joke with her that it would be hard for her to move back to the US because the pace is so different here. It's a very different lifestyle. But that is her journey and the life she has chosen to create.

And there are many days when I yearn for an intermission.

## THERE IS BEAUTY IN EVERY JOURNEY

When you look at the world, don't expect others to be just like you. By the same token, we should never push our beliefs or desires onto someone else. Everyone is different, and we need to let them be who they are. What works for me is definitely not going to work for the majority of people. My sister's life is very different than mine, and I doubt she would want to trade. Sure, it's nice to visit once in a while, but I think I have a pretty great life exactly where I am, and she has a pretty great life exactly where she is. The things that I enjoy and find comfort in are my fulfillment. Know what makes you happy, and what works for you. Don't let someone else persuade you into being who you are not. And don't focus on the comparison with others. The journey is the destination.

*Chapter 5*

# MORE THAN ONE PERSPECTIVE

## A NEW PAIR OF GLASSES

I've done a lot of things in my life, probably because I can't make a decision on what I want to be when I grow up. I was a CPA and then I owned a horse farm. Then I went back to school to be a teacher, and after that I worked in medical sales. Everything I've done has been an important part of my journey. I've traveled many paths that have finally led me to this moment in time. I'm now an author with a passion for public speaking. I'm sharing my story and making a difference one reader and one audience at a time. I'm finally where I belong—and where I was always meant to be.

There have been many stories that have enlightened me along the way. And one of those stories came while I was teaching. After I completed my teaching certificate and passed my exams, I was hired as a full-time substitute at a school that was a half hour away from my home. As a mom of six kids, I was used to all different kinds of personalities and knew to always expect the unexpected. There was a girl, whom I'll call "Hannah," in my fourth-grade class who was definitely smart, but was also really shy and super quiet. Two months into the school year, I noticed that Hannah had been absent for several days in a row. I was concerned because, although she had a few absences, it was unusual for her to miss so many days at once. I went to the principal's office to see what she knew about the absences.

During my conversation with the principal, I learned that Hannah's parents were arrested and that she was living in a teen shelter. My heart sank. I couldn't imagine my sweet fourth-grader in a shelter with teenagers. She was only ten years old. At the time there wasn't a shelter for children and toddlers in our community, and without any available foster placements, and with no family to speak of, Hannah really had nowhere to go.

I walked out of the principal's office knowing exactly what I wanted to do. I immediately called Rob and I said, "What do you think?"

He didn't even have to think about it. "Sure," he said.

I raced back to the principal's office and told her that we

would be willing to take Hannah until they could sort things out with her parents. Luckily, we still had the home study in place from Mili's adoption, and it was less than a year old. I spoke with the social worker, and he was willing to give it a shot. Hannah truly had no one else to take her in at that moment in time. By that afternoon, she was on her way to our house.

I still remember the black sedan pulling into the driveway. The social worker opened the left rear passenger door and Hannah stepped out. I walked down the steps to meet her. I could see a sense of relief on her face as she saw me. She had no idea where he was taking her. The only thing she was told was that she was not going to have to spend another night in the teen shelter. I hugged her and offered to help her carry her things. She didn't need any help because everything she had fit in a 12"x12" small cardboard box. I had to hold back my tears.

## ALREADY PART OF THE FAMILY

Everything happened so fast that we actually didn't tell the kids until right before she came over.

"There's a little girl in my class whose parents were arrested, and she doesn't have a place to go," I said. "Dad and I talked about it, and I know we didn't vote, but we'd like to let her stay with us for as long as she needs."

Not one of them had anything negative to say about letting Hannah come and stay with us. When they saw us walking up the steps with her cardboard box, Emma whispered, "Oh my gosh! Really? Is that all she has?"

My eyes closed for one-point-five seconds, and all I could think of to say was, "I know."

"Can we take her to Target tonight and get her whatever sheets she wants for her bed, and whatever clothes she needs, so that she feels like she's not just going to be here for two days and then gone again? She needs to feel like she has something of her own." This was a compilation of comments from the troops.

I truly have the best kids. They saw a little girl who just had her world flipped upside down and the rug torn from under her. They wanted to try to at least help her feel just a little bit better—create a bit of "normal." So, we went to Target where she picked out a zebra-striped comforter and some clothes.

Hannah lived with us for nine months. During that time, we learned so much about her life and what she had been through. Hannah had been bounced around quite a bit. But just prior to living with us, she had been living with her dad and his new wife, and four half-siblings. Her stepmom had just given birth prematurely to twins.

On the night Hannah was taken into custody, she was awakened to banging on the apartment door. She had no idea what was happening. She cautiously opened the door, and the police rushed in. The two preemies were in the crib, left without being connected to their heart-rate monitors. Hannah's younger sister was sleeping on the floor. Her brother, with a fever of 102, was found lying in a pool of vomit on the couch. Empty beer bottles, fifths of vodka, and used hypodermic needles lined the kitchen counters. Her dad and stepmom had been arrested at 2:00 a.m. at a local gas station. They were acting suspicious, and when questioned by police, they said they had to get home to the babysitter.

Hannah was the babysitter they were talking about, although she never knew they had even left the house. She was ten years old. She wasn't the babysitter—she was the daughter and the big sister.

For the first three months at our house, she would shower in her bathing suit, sleep with the lights on, and keep everything packed in the suitcase that we bought her in case she had to leave. I'm sure she was just waiting for the next time someone told her that she had to move again.

We took her to the dentist where she had multiple teeth pulled because they were rotten. We took her to the eye doctor, and I had a ridiculous teacher moment when I realized that the reason she sat so close to the front of the room wasn't because she really liked me, but because she couldn't see the board. When she put on her new pair of glasses, it was as if she was seeing the world for the very first time.

It wasn't just the new pair of glasses that opened Hannah's eyes. During the nine months that she stayed in our home, she became good friends with our kids. Not only did she impact the lives of my children, but they also left an impression on her. I believe seeing what it truly means to be loved by your family, and to be cared for, was a completely new perspective for her. It was something that she needed to see and experience for herself.

After nine months and many visitations, Hannah's grandmother got custody of her. We wanted her to stay, but that's not how the system works. Before she left, I sat down with her and told her how special she was. She wasn't only enough—she was more than enough. I told her that she was strong. I reminded her that she didn't have to do things that she knew were wrong, just because someone told her to. She deserved to be loved. She was kind, smart, and her opinion mattered. My hope was that the nine months in our home made a difference in her life. I hoped that she left knowing that we loved her.

What I do know is that she wasn't the only one who saw the world from a new perspective because of that experience.

## IT ALL BEGINS WITH THE ONE

Life is all about perspective. There's much good we can do for the world if we choose to see things from a different perspective.

We often think we're too insignificant or too unimportant to make a difference. That couldn't be further from the truth. Take the time to do something that will make a difference in someone else's life. It doesn't have to be much, and they don't even need to know what you've done for them. Just take a moment. Do something special. Make a difference.

Have you heard of the starfish story? If you don't know the story, this is how it goes. There once was an old man who used to come to the beach to do his writing. He liked to walk the beach before he started his work. He arrived at the beach one morning after a large storm had passed. The beach was covered with starfish, as far as the eye could see. He saw a young boy off in the distance. The boy seemed to stop every so often, bend down, and throw something into the water. The old man was curious what the boy was doing, so he asked him.

"I'm throwing starfish back into the water," the boy replied. "They can't make it back into the water themselves, and if they stay in the sun, they're all going to die."

"You're just wasting your time, son," the old man responded.

"There are thousands of starfish on this beach, and your small effort isn't going to make a difference."

The boy smiled at the old man, picked up a starfish, and threw it as far as he could into the ocean. "Well, Mister," he said, "I reckon it made a difference to that one." And the boy continued on his way, making a difference—one starfish at a time.

This is a perfect story about perspective. The old man was probably on the beach every day. Because of his age, he had seen a lot of things and had a lot of experiences. But because of those experiences, he saw the world in a certain way. The young boy, on the other hand, didn't have a lot of experience. He saw the world and the beach with fresh eyes. Instead of seeing the problem as overwhelming, he concentrated his efforts on what he could do, and focused on just one starfish at a time.

One starfish, one person, one issue: the story of the starfish is such a great reminder that seemingly small actions can make a huge difference. And when others see our efforts, they realize that they can make a difference too. Together, we can do so much good if we learn to see things differently.

## YOUR PERSPECTIVE IS YOUR PERSPECTIVE

In the story of the starfish, it's important to remember that the old man was taught an important lesson by the young boy. They both had their own perspective, but those perspectives were very different from each other.

As we travel along our life's journey, we may look at the world and mistakenly believe that we are always right, and that our perspective is the only perspective, and maybe even the best perspective. As a mother of six, I can tell you that we have many different perspectives in our house, and we can learn a lot from each other. I can't even begin to explain how much I've learned by seeing the world through my children's eyes.

We can't let our experiences sway us into thinking that there is only one way to see the world, or even a situation. When we are biased to our own way of looking at things, we forget that there is more than one perspective.

## LIFE LESSONS FROM ETHIOPIAN CHILDREN

I think one of the most powerful moments for me in understanding the value of a different perspective was when we were in the rural villages of Ethiopia. We were surrounded by poverty, yet everywhere we looked, the people seemed incredibly happy.

I remember thinking to myself, "Wait, why are people walking around so happy? How could they be happy living like this?" There was so much poverty, and what I saw was hardship. But I was looking at their world from my own experiences and perspective.

Their perspective was much different than mine. This was their life, and it was all that they had ever known. They didn't see it any other way, and their perspective was exactly right for them. What I saw as challenges were just their facts of life. They would wake up in the morning, do the work they needed to do, and celebrate the food on the table at night. Their focus was on survival—simply living one day at a time. That was their way of life. Was their life hard? Yes—but they were genuinely happy with it.

Sometimes, what we see as a problem isn't really a problem at all. If we look at the world through our own perspective, and forget that there are other perspectives, we may rush in to solve a problem, only to find that there was never really a problem to solve.

Initially, I looked at their way of life and thought that their lives would be so much better if they only had what we have. But in reality, our "stuff" hasn't made us any happier. Don't get me wrong, there are basic necessities that would improve their lives, like easy access to clean water, food, and shelter. But beyond those, they have very little want. Because from their perspective, they have all that they need.

As we traveled through the rural Ethiopian villages, we saw groups of children playing football, aka soccer. It is the most popular sport in Ethiopia. But in some of the most rural villages, their game was a bit different than any soccer game I had ever seen—mostly because they didn't have a soccer ball. Instead, they would take plastic bags and wad one up inside of the others, until it was one big plastic-bag ball. This is what they would use to kick around in their soccer game.

They loved their life, and they loved their "soccer ball." They had no idea that there was a different way of playing. They had just as much fun playing with their makeshift ball as any kid playing on the soccer field in our hometown. If we aren't careful, we can see something like that and think to ourselves, "How could that be fun? I need to get them a real soccer ball, so they can really know what they're missing."

But why do they need to know what we think they're missing when they're perfectly happy with what they already have? Instead, we can look at it and say, "Wow, I'm so impressed that they are using bags in that way, and they're having just as much fun as they would with a regular soccer ball." It's all about perspective.

It's about recognizing that when we move from one environment to the other, and travel from place to place, there are going to be so many different ways of seeing the world.

It's important that we remember not to push our views of the world on others, but respect where they are, especially when their perspective is different than our own.

Sometimes, in our desire to be the good in the world, we need to make sure that the good that we are doing is really what is needed. I could have given them a "real" soccer ball, but it wouldn't have solved a problem for them. They had already found a solution, and their plastic-bag ball was exactly perfect for what they needed.

Again, it's all about perspective.

## CHOOSE TO BE OPEN TO A NEW PERSPECTIVE

People often say, "Your kids are so lucky because you rescued them." It drives me crazy when I hear this, but I have to remember that people see things differently than I do. This is just their perspective.

When we adopted our children, they didn't even know that there was something different out there. Yes, they had unmet needs. But in my kids' perspective, they were just living their lives. In the orphanage, they were getting two meals a day, they played like children do, and they had love from their caretakers. To them, that was their normal, everyday life.

Many see them now and say that they are lucky children to have been adopted into our family. I say we are the lucky ones. They have added so much joy to our family. We have learned to find those things that bring us together, rather than focus on our differences. To us, it is our differences that make our family so special.

I don't see adoption as rescuing children. I see it as making the right choice when confronted with it. Making these choices has made all the difference in my life, because the world that has changed the most is my own.

## JUST DO YOUR BEST

When all is said and done, I truly believe that most problems in life are best understood when we choose to acknowledge that there are multiple perspectives to see them from. From a different perspective, large problems can be made small, and some things that we think are problems aren't really even problems at all.

As we move forward in our journey, we just have to remember that there are so many different ways to see things, and sometimes, we need to put on a new pair of glasses. We may not see things perfectly, because, after all, we're human. But as long as we are doing our best, we have the ability to make a positive difference in this world.

*Chapter 6*

# EVERYTHING HAPPENS FOR A REASON?

## THE POWER OF FAMILY

I was sitting in the lobby of the Mamounia hotel in Marrakesh, waiting to be seated for dinner, when my phone rang.

"Mom, Mom!" Olivia was hysterically screaming. "We were just in an accident!"

"Are you okay?" I asked.

She was sobbing so it was extremely difficult to understand what she was saying.

I repeated, "Are you okay?"

"I don't know if we're okay, Mom." That was the only answer they could give me.

Emma was driving Olivia to a dance at the school, when the car they were in was T-boned. Olivia was calling me from the scene of the horrific accident. It's the kind of call every parent fears when they're thousands of miles away from the scene of that accident. She just needed to be comforted more than anything. Fortunately, Emma was calling Rob on her phone. He was two minutes away and was rushing to get there.

I felt completely helpless. It was definitely one of those human moments when you realize just how quickly and suddenly life can change. I had no idea what was happening to my girls, and I had no way to get to them.

Rob arrived at the scene and was sick to his stomach when he saw the car. He said he didn't know how they survived it, and he refused to take a picture of it. But the twisted, broken metal somehow protected their lives. The EMTs examined the girls and said, "Emma has a broken arm, but Olivia looks fine." Rob looked at the car again and saw a spider-web crack in the passenger side of the windshield. He finished with the police, put the girls in the car, and drove to the emergency room.

My mom showed up at the hospital shortly after to help

care for my girls while I was away, and to keep me posted as to what was happening. Emma and Olivia were in two separate rooms. My mother described the tender scene to me and said that the girls spent most of their time moving back and forth between rooms to comfort each other. She watched Emma walk to Olivia's room where they would cry together as Emma apologized. "I'm sorry I almost killed you," she'd say, and they would cry some more.

Later, Olivia would walk to Emma's room and they would cry together again. "You can't feel bad, okay?" Olivia would tell Emma. Olivia has always had a really big heart.

The EMTs were correct about Emma. She had broken her right arm. But Olivia wasn't fine. She had fluid in her abdomen, and they transferred her to All Children's Hospital in Tampa. They quickly realized that she also had a severe concussion. As Rob suspected, she hit her head on the windshield, even though she was buckled.

I knew Emma would be struggling with what was happening with Olivia and would feel responsible because that's just who she is. Emma has the kindest soul. She worries about others and cares deeply. I knew this must be hard on her, yet there was nothing I could do from where I was at. I was hysterical. I had one kid at one hospital and another kid an hour away at another hospital, and I was still thousands of miles away from both of them.

I desperately tried to get home, but I couldn't. At the time, there was an airline on strike, and there were no available seats on any other flight out of Morocco. I spent two hours on the phone with the airline and made zero progress. All I could do was wait the four days until my flight was scheduled to leave. Enter extreme motherly guilt. But my family didn't see it that way. The girls were adamant that I didn't need to come home. Their perspective was valuable to me since I couldn't get a flight out, anyway.

No matter what I do, I always feel like I can and should do more. If I could be in three places at the same time, I would. But that isn't reality. What I realized in that moment was that I didn't need to be everything to everyone. The whole point of a family is that everyone contributes, and everyone has a role. Although I felt immense guilt for not being there, my family had it covered. They can handle anything put in front of them.

## ACCEPT THE UNFAMILIAR

Life is the best teacher. Oftentimes, life will present us with new experiences that will test us and give us the opportunity to grow. We can either embrace these new opportunities or stay in our comfort zone. But it's those new and unfamiliar opportunities that always provide the greatest growth. Adoption certainly pushed us out of our comfort zone, but we are better people because of it. In the end, we have to remember that everything that comes to us in our journey happens for a reason.

When we first met Ari, he would completely shut down when he was faced with any difficult situation. It was a coping mechanism for him. I can only imagine the difficulties he had faced in his early years, and as a result, Ari's only way of dealing with hard things was to completely shut down. His eyes would glaze over, and he would just sit there and stare into space, and we couldn't do anything to pull him out of it.

The first time we saw him shut down was at the orphanage. One of the nannies kept trying to feed him rice, literally stuffing it into his mouth. He refused to eat it. This kid was completely malnourished, but refused to eat rice. He proceeded to stare at the wall for about two hours. There was nothing that we could do to change what was happening. We just had to wait it out.

Ari's shutting down was a pretty big theme for the first year of him being home. We couldn't and wouldn't get upset with him. Not only was he a child, but we had no idea what he had been through to cause him to have such an extreme reaction to things. Most of the time, he shut down because he didn't like what was happening, or he didn't understand something that was happening to him.

The hardest part of this experience was when we enrolled

him in school. We felt that putting him immediately into school would really help him adjust and immerse him in the language. I can only imagine what must have been going on in his head. Here we had just taken him from the orphanage—a place with a lot of children and few adults—where he had been left by his father. And we were dropping him off at school—a place with a lot of children and few adults—and leaving him there. He didn't speak the language.

Although school was certainly nothing like the orphanage, in his mind it was exactly the same, and it caused him to shut down. I would walk him into the classroom, and every day I would say, "I promise, I'm coming back. I will always come back." But I'm sure he still didn't understand what was happening. How could he? What child could understand what had happened over the last few months of his life? What adult could persevere in those same circumstances? He would literally lie by the door and wait until I came back for him.

Introducing Ari to school was a growing experience for both Ari and the rest of us. We felt Ari needed school, but he didn't even understand what school was. We were all in an unfamiliar situation, and because of this, we learned how to move through change together.

## LEAN IN

One morning, after I got Ari up and dressed, I then focused on getting the other kids up and ready. But when I went downstairs to make breakfast, I couldn't find Ari anywhere. I panicked and started screaming his name, "Ari! Ari!" which I'm sure probably scared the absolute crap out of him. He probably thought he was in trouble and that I was upset with him, because why else would someone scream? But I was completely panicking!

Thinking back on that experience, I am sure it was traumatizing for him, even though I was truly only concerned with his welfare. I don't know what his life was like before he came to our house. All I know is that when he cried, he cried with silent tears.

I went outside, desperately looking for him. I looked in the pool. I looked in the canal. I went through every place I could think of outside and inside the house. I was totally freaking out and felt physically sick to my stomach.

Finally, in a complete panic, I called my mom. "You have to come over," I said. "I can't find Ari anywhere! If we can't find him, I'm going to have to call the police." That was my next step. All I could think of was that Ari had only been with us for a couple of weeks, and I had already lost him.

When my mom came over, we scoured the house again.

It had been two hours since anyone had seen him, and my heart was sinking. We finally found him lying under the dining room table, under the curtains, at the perfect angle where he couldn't really be seen. I ran to him. He had totally shut down again and looked scared to death. But I pulled him into my arms and hugged him. I am sure this was equally as confusing to him. I was yelling his name, then hugging him. He didn't understand, but I wanted him to know he was safe.

Although Ari tried to hide so he wouldn't have to go to school, we still felt that school was the right place for him. He wasn't afraid of school. He was afraid that we wouldn't come back for him. For two months, he would lie at that door waiting for me—and for two months, I would promise him I was coming back. Every day when I came back, he had a huge smile on his face. It was me building up trust and helping him know that I would always come back for him.

Ari's behavior of shutting down whenever something unknown happened continued. But over time, it started getting better. Not only was the frequency going down, but the intensity was going down as well. Instead of him staring off into space for two hours, it became an hour and a half. And at school, he moved from lying by the door to lying down in the classroom.

Eventually, when he really understood the language and

he tried to shut down, I would say, "Ari, we're not shutting down. You have to use your words and tell me what's wrong, because we can fix it if you will just tell me. But if you shut down, there is nothing we can do to help make things better."

Finally, after about a year, instead of shutting down, he would say, "I don't like that," or, "I don't want to eat that because..." Having the ability to use his words made all the difference.

Even school got easier for him. When the director came to me and said, "It's great we have Ari in the classroom now, but he doesn't participate, he just lays there," I asked, "Have you talked to him about it?"

"Not really," she said.

I walked over to Ari and said, "Ari, can you stop lying down in the classroom and sit down and talk with the other kids?"

"Okay," he said. And that was the end of it. It was just one of those things that required asking. Sometimes we don't realize how easy the answer can be or how simple the solution actually is because we don't ask the question. Ari also had to make up his mind that school was okay and that I was always going to come back for him. After that, he was fine. He made friends and he loved school.

When I think of Ari's story, I think of all the times in our own lives where we shut down because we are faced with something new. If we remember that everything happens for a reason and remind ourselves that change is often a good thing, we can stop ourselves from resisting those changes and lean in to them when they come.

Ari had no idea he was resisting—he just didn't understand. But there are times when you or I may resist opportunities on purpose because we're comparing them to our past experiences. But knowledge is power, and experience is the best teacher. School was not the orphanage. Once Ari recognized that for himself, he was finally able to grow and embrace the new opportunities school gave him.

So many times, we resist new opportunities because we can't get over our past experiences. I will be the first one to admit that it is hard to view new situations without putting them in the framework of our past experiences. It's not easy to start dating again once you have had a broken heart. It is difficult to get back in a car again after a major accident. And it is tough to try again when you feel you have failed. Because of this, we sometimes give up great opportunities in the present because we are afraid of what happened in the past.

When Ari walked into that classroom, there is no doubt in my mind that he thought I was leaving him at another orphanage. But because he kept going—and I kept coming back—little by little, he was finally able to see the good in it, and now he is thriving.

Our greatest growth can come when we stop resisting the experiences life throws at us and lean in to the opportunities that change us for the better. Embrace those things that come. After all, everything happens for a reason.

## EACH ADOPTION HAPPENED FOR A REASON

As a family, we had to lean into our adoption experience. Our lives drastically changed, and it wasn't always an easy road to travel. Some people think that adopting children is all sunshine and roses. While I wholeheartedly believe that all children are amazing, whether you give birth to them or not, there is nothing that is a fairy tale about adoption. It is work.

It is hard work to even just get through the day sometimes. These kids have suffered so much loss. You basically start at that point of heartache and loss and move forward. You can't make up for what they've lost—you just can't. They have gone through things that most people will never experience. To compare it to anything else is almost impossible.

Adoption is never an easy decision. The process is a difficult one for everyone involved, from the adopting family, to the family giving up their rights to their own child—and it's especially difficult for the child who has to adjust to a whole new way of living. We didn't take the decision lightly because we understood the impact it would have on our household and the children we were bringing into our family.

But I can say that, without a doubt, every child in our family is a vital part, and there is a reason they are here. Sometimes we know the reason immediately, and sometimes those reasons become apparent over time. But every time we have added a missing piece to our family, the reasons become very apparent as to why they were meant to be a part of our family.

### EMBRACE CHANGE

Take Ari, for example. When he was young, he obviously suffered huge losses in his life. His biological mother died when he was a toddler. He was left at an orphanage because his family literally didn't have enough food to feed everyone in their household; he was malnourished when we adopted him. I can't even imagine how scary it must have been for him to lose everything he had known and then become part of a new family. But I truly believe that he is right where he is supposed to be and that he is part of the family that he's supposed to be in.

Although he suffered huge losses, Ari has gained so many

opportunities that would have never been possible if adoption was not part of his journey. He has access to great schools and an education that would not have been possible in Ethiopia. His life in Ethiopia was about survival. Even at the age of four, Ari was helping to take care of the family's livestock and crops. The focus was on making it through the day and having enough to eat. Many days, there wasn't enough food for everyone in his family. That's not something he has to ever worry about here.

But even here, there are still remnants of his past. When he was little and I traveled for work, he used to insist that I wake him up before I left for the airport. He never wanted to miss the opportunity to say goodbye. I once made the mistake of not waking him up before I left. It was two o'clock in the morning and he just looked so peaceful. I called when I landed and he wouldn't speak to me. Actually, he wouldn't speak to me for three days. He had been through so much. He asked one small thing of me and I didn't follow through. Lesson learned. I've learned so much in my journey as Ari's mother.

Ari has dyslexia and dysgraphia, but that hasn't slowed him down. He has learned to self-advocate, which is one of the most important skills anyone can have. He has access to resources, tutors, and individualized help. His teachers love him because he's willing to work hard, and he is kind to everyone he meets. Ari has excelled in school and has also found success in athletics, where he is a natural born leader.

When Ari was in the eighth grade, I once got a text from his tutor who worked with him after school. This is what it said: "I want to tell you, because Ari probably won't, LOL. The coach said the nicest things to Ari today about being a leader in lacrosse. He thanked him for his patience with the sixth graders and complimented his overall athleticism. His words were so kind and true. It made me start to choke up. What a gift to Ari. Of course, he pretended like it was no big deal. He was also so polite and said thank you numerous times. Just in case he doesn't tell you."

It's moments like these, when Ari gets to shine because of who he is, that remind me of what a gift his adoption has been for our family. Everything that has happened in his life has made him such a strong person and a great leader. In truth, everything that has happened to him has brought him to the exact place he needs to be.

Some people may say, "He doesn't get to be with his birth family," but that wasn't our decision. The choice we made was to make him a part of our family and to love him. What I can say is that because of the gift his birth family gave us, Ari truly has been able to shine, and he has changed our lives forever.

Every time something happens in your journey, and every choice you make to embrace change, is putting you on the path to becoming a better version of who you are.

## DON'T WORRY, BE HAPPY

Even though I am a strong proponent of "Everything happens for a reason," I know full well that things will happen in our lives that can cause us to spin out of control. We can end up worrying ourselves sick, if we aren't careful—especially if the things that happen seem less of an opportunity for growth, and more of a difficult hardship. Because while it's true that life gives us opportunities, it also gives us hardships.

It's especially important when these hardships come to remember that everything happens for a reason. Things will happen in your life that you can't do anything about. If you spin your wheels focusing on those things that you can't do anything about, you will end up making yourself miserable. Worrying about things is not going to do anyone any good, so just don't do it.

For me, I try to look at things with a more positive perspective. That makes a lot of difference in my ability to get through those hard things. For example, when we are in the car and there has been an accident, and everyone else is frustrated because we are late to something, I remind them to be glad that we weren't the ones in the accident. We are still able to make it to where we are going, just a little later than we expected, rather than riding in an ambulance on the way to the emergency room.

So many times, we ask, "Why did this happen to me?" Every time I have moved forward in my journey and looked backward, there has always been a reason. Even when people say that they can't see the reason, there probably is one—they just don't see it. The whole point of this is that you can't just give up because things turn out differently than you expected, or because you don't get what you want in that moment. There are going to be many more moments. Learn from it and move forward.

We may never know why things happen the way they do, but we can be certain that they happen for a reason.

*Chapter 7*

# IT'S OKAY TO BE HUMAN

## A SNAKE IN THE HOLE

One Friday night, while I was in Israel leading a mission for the Jewish Federation, I received an urgent call from Rob.

"Noah has been bit by a poisonous snake," he said. "And I don't know what the status is." At the time, Noah was attending a summer camp in Georgia. He had been attending that camp for the past month and was scheduled to be home the following Monday, only three days away. "I just finished operating and I'm going straight from the hospital to get on a plane to fly to Atlanta," Rob said. "I'll call you later."

"What?" I yelled. My heart sank and my mind started swimming. I had no idea how to respond to that, and I was having a hard time processing what was happening. I was so far away from everyone and wanted more information.

"I can't talk," Rob said. "I literally have to run to get on the plane. Call the camp."

And with that, he hung up the phone, and I was left in a frantic mess.

There was so little I could do from Israel, but I needed to understand what was actually happening, in real time. I did what Rob suggested and I called the camp. I told them who I was and asked if they could connect me to the clinic. They immediately transferred me.

I spoke to the pediatrician who was on call, as well as the assistant camp director. They both basically told me the same thing, "We're taking every precaution. We don't think it was poisonous, but just in case, we're putting him in an ambulance and taking him down the mountain to the closest emergency room to get him checked out."

In my mind, I kept thinking that this is what they would tell any mom, "Don't worry, we have it under control, and everything is going to be fine." They set up a WhatsApp group to keep us in the loop. But other than that, there was nothing I could say or do that would make the situation better, and I couldn't get home if I wanted to.

I hung up the phone, still crying hysterically. They may have said that he was fine, but in my mind, the fact that they were putting him in an ambulance was not a good sign.

Not even fifteen minutes later, I received another phone call. "Well, um, we just wanted to let you know that things have changed a little bit," the assistant director said. "As we were taking him down in the ambulance, his arm got much more swollen. So, we decided to put him in a helicopter. The ambulance is now headed to the closest private airport and the helicopter is meeting them there."

With this new information, it was as if the whole world was spinning around me. I just wanted to be there for my son. I could only imagine what he was going through all alone, without me or Rob there to comfort him. "Well, can you tell me who's with him?" I asked. "Is somebody from the camp with him?"

"Yeah, the nurse from the camp is with him," she said.

"Can I have her phone number?" I asked. I just needed to know that Noah was okay and that he was not alone. I felt that if I couldn't be there with him, the next best thing I could do was to talk to and through someone who was with him.

I called the nurse, and as she was giving me the update, I abruptly stopped her and said, "Can I ask you a favor? Can you talk to me as a mom? Don't talk to me as a camp employee; just talk to me as a mom. I need to know the truth." I could just tell that there was something they weren't telling me. And I wanted to know the truth. The truth is much easier to deal with than the what-ifs that kept coming up in my thoughts. I just wanted her to tell me like it was, no sugarcoating it.

She got quiet and then said, "As a mom, this is scaring the shit out of me. He went from his arm being almost normal, to completely like a balloon in fifteen minutes. The reason we're putting him on a helicopter is that we're worried about compartment syndrome, where it gets so swollen that it shuts off the blood supply, and then they'll have to open up the skin so that the swelling goes down. That's our biggest concern, and we are doing all we can to avoid it. That's why we're getting on a helicopter right now." I could tell she was freaking out too.

"Okay," I said. Of course, it was scary to hear, but it was better for me to know exactly what was happening, than for everyone to pretend that everything was fine. After I knew the reality of the situation, I was better able to manage my fear. I'm not exactly sure why, but I work better knowing what I'm facing.

## THROUGH THE EYES OF A CHILD

The helicopter life-flighted Noah to the hospital, and an hour and a half later, Rob arrived. When he walked into the ICU, sitting with Noah was our rabbi, who had been at the summer camp with his kids and made a four-hour drive to the hospital to sit with Noah until Rob arrived. It was such a comfort for Rob and me to both know that our son was being taken care of, especially when we couldn't be there ourselves. Noah was tiny, and he had been bit twice by the snake, and given how quickly his arm swelled, we feared the worst.

Noah was in the ICU for two nights receiving several vials of anti-venom. They had determined that it was either a copperhead or a rattlesnake. Since both have the same antivenom, they were able to neutralize the venom and stop it from spreading.

While in the hospital, the camp called Rob and let him know that they had found the snake and killed it. When Rob told Noah, he was visibly upset about it.

"That makes me really sad," Noah said. "It wasn't the snake's fault, it was mine. I put my hand into its home to get my ball back. It wasn't trying to hurt me. It wasn't like it was coming after me. It's just that I reached into an area where it was, and I scared it. That's why it bit me. It was just trying to protect itself, and it didn't deserve to die."

I am always learning so much by seeing things through the eyes of my children. Even though the snake almost killed Noah, he was sad that the snake had been killed instead. In his mind, the snake was just doing what snakes do—it was scared and struck out. That understanding allowed him to have compassion for the snake. Likewise, humans are... well, human. Perhaps if we saw ourselves simply as humans being human, we would have a little more compassion for ourselves and others.

By Sunday night, Noah was doing well enough that they were ready to release him.

Rob suggested to Noah that they just fly home, "Well, you know, your sister can just bring your bags back with her and we can just fly home."

"No, I don't want to miss the last night at camp," Noah said.

"Seriously?" Rob asked.

"Yeah, I want to go back. Please, I want to go back."

They wrapped up his arm, and Noah went back to camp. Rob and Noah stayed in a room off of the nurse's room. Noah got to participate with the campers for the night, and they flew home the next morning. And Noah became the cool kid.

## I SMELL A RAT

When everyone got back home, we made an appointment with the physical therapist right away. Noah's arm was locked in place at a ninety-degree angle, because of the swelling, and he couldn't straighten it at all. We hoped that the physical therapist could help Noah regain full range of motion in his elbow.

We got into our minivan (aka, moving trashcan) to go to the therapist. It was our first time in that car for at least a two-week period.

"Buckle up," I said to Noah.

"It's kind of hard because I only have one arm," he said.

"I know; just buckle," I said back to him.

I could see from the rearview mirror that he was trying his best to buckle his seatbelt. "Are you buckled?" I asked, turning my head back to see if he was for sure buckled.

"Buckled," he said.

But while my head was turned, my attention wasn't so much on his answer as it was on the popcorn that was spread all over the seats and the floor.

"Noah, why is the popcorn all over the seat?" I asked.

"I don't know," he shrugged.

"I swear I cleaned the car before we left," I said.

I started to back the car out of the garage, but I couldn't get the image of the popcorn out of my mind. Something just didn't seem right about it. I kept looking at the popcorn while still trying to focus on backing out the car. Halfway out of the garage and into the driveway, it hit me hard—that's not popcorn!

"Noah! Get out of the car!" I yelled.

"What?" he asked. I'm sure he was both surprised and scared because of the urgency in my voice.

"Get out of the car, now!" I yelled even louder.

As we got out of the car, I looked closer at the "popcorn" that was covering nearly every inch of our car. Only it wasn't popcorn; it was the inside fluff of the seats. Almost every seat had chunks out of it, and rat poop was everywhere. I don't know if it was one rat, two rats, or a family of them. But somehow, rats had gotten into our car, probably through the engine block, and had a feast. I'm sure they were in heaven because, with six kids, there were probably crackers shoved in every nook and cranny of that minivan, and those rats made sure they found every last crumb. They chewed on nearly every seat in the car. And what they left in their food raid was absolutely disgusting!

The first thing I did was call my pest-control guy. He set some traps in the van and suggested that I call my insurance company. At this point, I hadn't seen a need to involve the insurance company, as I was still thinking that everything would be fine. We would just get it cleaned, and all would be well.

A day went by and the rat traps remained empty, so I called my insurance company. Imagine that conversation: "Yes, could you please tell me if our car insurance covers rats?"

I'm pretty sure they didn't take me seriously when I explained the damage, but they were nice about it. "Well, okay," he said. "We'll have it looked at. Why don't you drive it over to the insurance adjuster?"

"Yeah, right, I'm not driving it." I said. Again, it was probably hard for them to understand the state of the minivan, until they witnessed it for themselves. But it wasn't just the mess that bothered me; it was the fact that there could still be a rat in there.

"Well, why not?" he said. "It's still drivable, right? There's nothing wrong with the engine."

"Yeah," I said, "and there's a rat or seven in there. What if it jumps on my head while I'm driving to the repair place? I'm not doing that. Because then I'll have a complete freak-out that will lead to an accident, and then it will be more expensive for you guys. Not to mention I will be trauma-tized for life."

"Yeah, I guess you're right," he said. "I'll have someone come tow it."

After they towed the minivan to the shop, I got a phone call from the appraiser. "I have to tell you," he said, "I've done this for over twenty years, and I have never seen anything like this before. I actually don't even know where to begin. I'll get back to you in a couple of days because I've got to look up all the costs of this."

All I could do was laugh at his response and wait for his call.

A few days later his call came. "I hate to tell you this," he said, "but it will cost so much to fix your minivan that I have to total it." He laughed as he said, "Never in my life did I ever think that I would say I totaled a car because a rat ate the seats. But I'm totaling your car because a rat ate the seats."

A rat totaled our minivan—I'm one of few people who can say that with a straight face.

## RECOGNIZING OUR IMPERFECTION

We all have days like this. It may not be rats in the minivan, but we all have our human days, because we are all human. To be honest, every day is a human day, and that is perfectly okay. Because, unlike the pictures you see on social media, nobody's life is perfect.

Sure, there are many people who make their living as an influencer on social media. Some make millions of dollars promoting beauty brands, posting reaction videos, and vlogging. The more followers they have, the more brands want to use them to advertise their products. But these people we see aren't perfect, and neither is their message.

Social media has shown us the power of both information and misinformation. The ability to connect with people and disseminate information quickly to large groups is probably one of the most powerful pieces of the internet today. The problem is that there is so much information that it can be difficult to comb through and figure out what is real and what is fake. As parents, we focus on teaching our kids that the people on social media aren't perfect and what they share is often their own opinion. We remind them that they should never simply accept what they are shown on social media, but actually educate themselves on a topic instead.

Just like social influencers, we're all imperfect people. Yet, many of us strive to only post the great stuff on social media, leaving others to believe that our life is the picture of perfection. But a photo is only one moment in a thousand. We may see someone's perfect moment on social media, but what we don't see is what happened before the photo or what happened after the photo. We don't see the thousands of human moments that happen around and between the one perfect moment that was posted.

Those perfect pictures are a lot like our minivan. From the outside, it looked totally fine, but on the inside, it was obviously a complete and total disaster. I'm not implying that people's lives are complete and total disasters, but we often tend to post our best selves instead of our real selves.

Recently, I had a photograph taken of all our kids together in one location—without the assistance of photoshop. When people look at it, they tell me how amazing it is and how lucky I am to have kids who just sit and smile for the camera. They didn't see the other five thousand photos that the photographer took where the kids were pushing each other and complaining. I chose to share the one moment out of thousands that had the image I wanted people to see.

That's how social media is. It isn't reality, but we still use it to compare our own life to others' lives.

We're human. We're not supposed to be perfect. To be honest, I don't strive for perfection, because that's not reality. I strive to be the best me I can be. And the best me is still human and full of flaws. Those flaws are a part of me, and I learn so much from them. I am sure that others learn from my flaws too. Some of the most inspiring people to me are the people who expose their flaws. They don't try to pretend that they're perfect, because they know that nobody is.

It's okay to be human. We learn from our mistakes.

My daughter had a first-grade teacher who actually celebrated when they made mistakes, because mistakes meant that they were learning. They would clap and sing and then correct the mistake. Every kid in that class was willing to raise their hand and take a risk because they knew they wouldn't be ridiculed for making a mistake.

Everybody is different. We have different strengths and weaknesses—that's what being human is about. It's important that we accept our own humanness and be happy with where we are.

We are all going to have ridiculous moments in our lives—moments where we question our own sanity and our ability to accomplish even the littlest of things. Life is not going to be easy all of the time, but that's what makes it a journey. We never know what lies ahead. All we can do is face our adventure with courage and keep a good sense of humor.

When those ridiculous moments happen, we are faced with a choice. As I said before, we can choose to make ourselves miserable, or we can choose to figure out a solution. And even if there is no solution, misery is still totally optional. Sure, there are days where I just want to sit and be miserable about something. But then I remember that those things are outside of my control. I make the choice to do the things I can, and to stop being miserable over those things that I can't do anything about it.

## OUR HUMAN JOURNEY

In this human journey of ours, not only will we have ridiculous moments, but we will all face the kind of challenges that will make us question our abilities. When we have those challenges, I have learned that the best thing we can do is to rise to the occasion by focusing on what matters most and letting go of all the things we cannot change. Often, one of the hardest things for us to do is to accept the challenging things that happen in life. But they are going to come, and we have to be ready for them, even if they take us off guard. When these difficult types of challenges come, we have to embrace what just might seem to break us and keep moving forward anyway. My dad getting sick was definitely one of those challenges for me.

My dad grew up in Israel. He was there when Ben Gurion gave his famous speech declaring the State of Israel. He was in the Israeli Defense force. And when his family moved back to Germany to try to reclaim their life, he joined them there—because family always came first.

My dad was a very intelligent man. They only spoke Hebrew at home, so he moved to Germany without even knowing the German language. He had a desire to attend medical school, and not knowing the language wasn't going to deter him from his goal. His father had to translate for him at his medical school interview, and he was accepted. Despite having to learn German while dealing with the rigors of medical school, he had the second highest GPA in his class— which was totally irritating to him because he wasn't first. That's so like him, though. He was always a good example to me of dedication, perseverance, and believing in yourself.

In September 2017, my dad was diagnosed with stage four adenocarcinoma of the lung. It had already spread throughout his body before we even knew he was sick. As a retired physician, he was always good about taking care of others, but he was the worst at taking care of himself. He constantly had a cough because of allergies. On one of his regular check-ups, he asked his physician if he could do a CT scan because his cough just wasn't letting up. He never felt sick; he only had a cough that wouldn't go away.

By the time we knew he was sick, the cancer had already spread throughout his body. He had it in his spine, in his pelvis, in his femur. It was unbelievable that he had such advanced disease, but few symptoms. There's often bone pain with this type of cancer. But he's a really, really tough guy, and he just thought it was the usual "getting older" kind of pain.

My dad's diagnosis was a huge shock for our family. I really struggled to accept it—we all did. But one of the most difficult aspects for me was watching my mom care for my dad after his diagnosis.

I love my mom. She's a fighter in her own right. She grew up in rural Pennsylvania on a small farm. They grew everything, canned everything, and ate everything they grew and canned. Her mother had a sixth-grade education, and her father worked in the coal mines and at a local brewery.

My mom saw a library for the first time in tenth grade. That was a turning point for her. She knew she wanted a higher education and had the grit to make it happen. She worked for a local family taking care of their kids, so that she could save up enough money to go to college. She worked her butt off and was admitted to the University of Pittsburgh in 1957.

My mom worked three jobs while in college. She was admitted to medical school at the University of Pittsburgh and graduated in 1965. There were one hundred and twenty people in her medical school class. One hundred and fifteen of them were men. She was one of five women. As a child I never considered boundaries in my decision-making because my mother had broken every ceiling.

As a wife, my mom always took care of my dad. She was the kind of companion who would leave a sandwich in the fridge for him when she knew she wouldn't be home at lunchtime. But the kind of care required for his cancer was all-consuming. I could tell it wasn't easy for her, but she never complained and cared for my dad to the very end.

He tried every treatment that was offered to him and fought hard for twenty months. Unfortunately, cancer is a horrible disease. It transforms the strongest of souls into the weakest of humans. In the end, you can't even care for yourself. I saw my dad cry just three times in his life: when his father died, when I left for college, and when he knew it was our last goodbye. He will always be the man I compare everyone to; he will always be the first man I ever loved. He will always be the best father my sister and I could have ever had. He will always be my dad, and I will always miss him. But I learned that even though his journey ended, I couldn't let his death stop me from moving forward in my own journey. He wouldn't want that.

Is it hard? Yes. Is it difficult to accept? Of course it is. It is terrible, it is painful, and it is life-changing. But it is, and always will be, a part of life. And we can't ever allow it to stop us from living. It's okay to cry and to be angry because we are human—but when we're ready, we have to pick ourselves up and keep moving forward.

When we have experiences like this in our life, the kind of experiences that are gut-wrenching and heartbreaking, we can either let them break us, or we can try to find the beauty that is waiting to be found. We would never understand the joy of life if we didn't also know the sorrow. Unfortunately, we can't seem to have one without the other.

Some journeys are long, some journeys are short, but every journey is a human journey that will be filled with ups and downs and everything in between. The trick is to embrace it all and to find joy in the journey.

**EMBRACE YOUR HUMANNESS**

No one is beyond the trials that come in life. Even the most intelligent and the most successful person you know struggles at times. They have human weaknesses, and human moments, just like everyone else.

My husband is the perfect example of this. He is a surgeon. In the operating room or the emergency room, he is focused and on top of his game. He has seen things in his profession that would make even the strongest person shudder. He is cool, calm, and collected, and he knows just what to do to save the lives of those he operates on. To me, he is the best at what he does. But when it comes to our kids, all of his training and experience goes out the window, and his humanness takes over.

When Olivia was three years old, we all went to Tuscany to attend the wedding of one of my closest friends. At the time, it was just Rob, me, and the three oldest kids. We hadn't yet adopted the younger three. Everyone who went to the wedding, close to forty people, stayed in the same villa together. One day, they invited us to a wine tasting. Rob encouraged me to go and said that he would take the kids into the village to go exploring. My friend's dad volunteered to go with Rob and the kids because he doesn't drink. I was excited that I could go to the wine tasting, and I didn't have to worry about the kids since they would be with Rob. I went on my way, and they made their way to the village.

When they got to the village, they tried to find a place to park. It was a walled city, and Rob didn't realize that cars weren't allowed within the city walls. He drove straight through an opening in the wall, turned, and kept going until the road became very, very skinny, and the car got smooshed. Luckily, we had purchased the full-coverage rental insurance on the car. Rob was able to back out and found a parking spot outside of the city. But by this time, he was frazzled because not only was the car in bad shape, but he had our three kids with him, and Olivia was screaming at the top of her lungs that she had to go to the bathroom. My friend's dad was there to witness all the chaos. I'm sure his emotions were a combination of laughter and terror as he watched the comedy of errors that was our life.

They looked for a restroom, and finally found one. The way this bathroom worked is you put in a coin, the door opens, you go in, the door closes, and you use the restroom. What Rob didn't realize is that, if the bathroom is in use, when the person comes out, the door closes first, the whole bathroom is washed down, and then you put your coin in and the door opens again. But that's not what happened.

A woman came out of the bathroom, Olivia ran in, the door closed, they heard the wash cycle start, and then they heard Olivia's blood-curdling screams. They couldn't get in no matter how hard they tried because the door locks during the wash cycle and doesn't open again until the wash cycle is complete. When the door finally opened, there was poor Olivia, completely traumatized and soaking wet from head to toe. Of course, at that point, she probably had already peed her panties, so it didn't really matter.

They did what they could to get her cleaned up and decided to continue to explore the village. The whole day, Olivia complained about her feet hurting, but they just figured it was because she was three and they were doing a lot of walking. They walked around for a few hours, until Olivia's clothes dried, and then they headed home.

When they got back to the villa, my friend's dad looked at Olivia and said, "Hey, Rob, do you know she has her shoes on the wrong feet?" Olivia had literally been walking around the entire day with her shoes on the wrong feet, because Rob had put them on that way. In the craziness and chaos that is often our life, he missed an important detail. Sometimes days like that just happen.

It's okay to be human. It was a really bad day with a series of unfortunate events. But the next day, life moved on. Olivia's feet were a little sore for a while, and she still says she's traumatized by the self-washing bathroom, but she laughs about it, and it is a day we will remember for the rest of our lives.

We are all going to have days like this. When they come, we need to accept our humanness and recognize that we are going to make mistakes. And that is okay, and even expected.

## HUMANS HAVE WEAKNESSES

This wasn't the only time Rob's humanness took over. Just like me, he has his own moments of weakness.

One night, Ari was outside fishing with a friend in the dark.

I was lying upstairs with Olivia when Mili came running in and said, "You gotta come down, Dad's calling for you! Something happened to Ari!"

"Oh, he's fine," Olivia said. "Let us finish our conversation."

"No, you have to go!" Mili said. "Something's really wrong."

When we ran downstairs, what we saw was a blood bath. There was so much blood that, after it was all said and done, Olivia used the hose to wash down our driveway. In her own words, it looked like someone had been "slaughtered."

Apparently, while trying to walk around a chair on the dock, Ari fell into the water and landed in an oyster bed, where an oyster lodged in the bottom of his foot. Ari was definitely in shock. He kept screaming, "I think I'm going to lose my foot. I think I'm going to lose my foot."

Rob was justifiably freaked out by the situation. As I said, Rob, as a physician, can handle any stressful situation. But

Rob, as a dad, sometimes panics and forgets that he's a doctor. It's the craziest thing.

After reassuring both of them that Ari was going to be okay, we ended up at the hospital.

Even though the shell was almost to the bone, and he had totally lacerated the tendons, Ari made a full recovery, after eight weeks of them cutting off the cast, checking for infection, and putting the cast back on again. It was a long process. But, incredibly, in the end, he didn't have any permanent damage.

There are other stories, like when Emma was little and decided to turn the couch into a slide and hit her head on the TV table. There was blood everywhere, and Rob was struggling to stay calm. Or the time when Mili threw a squirt gun at Noah and hit him directly between the eyes. Again, blood gushed out and Rob was in a fatherly panic. I had to step in to help calm everyone down and evaluate the situation.

Rob is a fantastic surgeon. He sees blood every day. But when that blood is coming from his own child, it becomes personal. It's like a switch is flipped and the dad inside the doctor comes out and his humanness takes over.

## BETTER TOGETHER

It's fascinating that the blood factor doesn't freak me out. But other things definitely do. I'm usually calm and collected during an emergency with the kids. Six kids means six times the emergencies, so you get used to the chaos. But I definitely have my own freak-out moments.

Before our trip to Italy, where Olivia was cleansed by the bathroom, she had been really sick with Rotovirus. We had spent three days before the trip in the hospital with her. When she was no longer contagious, the doctor discharged her and approved of her traveling to Italy with us.

I focused on Olivia the entire flight. I imagine Emma and Jacob watched movies all night and drank sugary caffeinated drinks because they knew I wasn't paying attention. When we landed in Rome, we spent the day exploring. We got to our hotel at five in the afternoon and couldn't keep our eyes open.

A few hours later I heard what I thought was the kids messing around. I rolled over, preparing myself to raise my voice. But when I opened my eyes, I saw something I will never get out of my mind. Jacob was having a seizure. His eyes rolled back in his head while his body twitched and postured. I lost it.

Rob jumped out of bed and completely took control of the

situation. Fortunately, after a few minutes, Jacob's body stopped posturing and Rob was making arrangements to get Jacob examined at a local hospital. I, on the other hand, was a wreck. I had never seen someone have a seizure before, and I couldn't wrap my head around the situation. I remember crying and saying, "I just want to go home."

Fortunately, Rob had it under control. Jacob's seizure was probably due to a combination of lack of sleep and way too many Coca Colas. Thankfully, that seizure was a one-time event for Jacob.

In emergency medical situations with our children, Rob and I both do our best. But there are moments when our humanness completely takes over. Fortunately, we don't seem to have these freak-out moments at the same time. We're always much better—together.

**PERFECTION NOT REQUIRED**

We all have our weaknesses. We all have things that we struggle with. But just because we struggle, doesn't mean we shouldn't do what we can. The more we accept our humanness, the more good we can do. Perfection isn't required. All that is required is our willingness to accept the things we cannot change and to do the good that we can.

Sometimes we'll get frustrated. Sometimes we'll freak out.

And sometimes we just need to have a sense of humor and laugh at ourselves. Even in the ridiculous moments, we all have something to give. It's our job to figure out what that is, and to go out there and do it.

You may feel like the odds are stacked against you, but I've learned from those who have come before me that you can do anything you set your mind to. You just have to believe you can.

*Chapter 8*

# YOU DON'T HAVE TO MOVE MOUNTAINS

## CLIMBING MOUNT KILIMANJARO

From a distance, Mount Kilimanjaro looked like a tiny speck. I remember sticking my thumb out, closing one eye, and the entire mountain disappeared. But the closer we got to it, the bigger it became. I, along with fifteen others, had come to climb the world's fourth-highest mountain, its peak rising from the Tanzanian rainforest to more than nineteen thousand feet above sea level. I don't think any of us realized exactly what we were getting ourselves into when we agreed to climb Mount Kilimanjaro to raise money for the Livestrong Foundation in their efforts to fight cancer. But there we were, sixteen strangers from all walks of life, ready to climb a mountain together.

Originally my husband was asked if he wanted to do it; I imagine he counted to three and then answered his colleague with, "No, thank you. Call Simone." And when I got the phone call, my answer was, "Absolutely!"

I had trained for six months to make this climb—a seven-day adventure of a lifetime. I was excited to be there not only to help a good cause, but to experience one of the toughest challenges I had ever signed up for. Standing at the base of the mountain, looking at the behemoth in front of me, I was overwhelmed by a mix of excitement and a little fear. But I've never backed down from a challenge, and I was determined to make it to the top.

## BEGINNING THE CLIMB

I was climbing with a group of people who were complete strangers to me, brought together by a common goal—to summit Mt. Kilimanjaro while raising funds and awareness for the Livestrong Foundation. Some were cancer survivors; others were climbing in honor of those who had lost the battle and those who were still fighting. I had no idea how these people worked by themselves, nor how they worked as a team. But every member of our team was there for a reason, and I knew it was going to be an amazing adventure.

Our climb of the Rongai route began outside of the national park. Our first campsite was in the tropical area of the mountain, so everything was green and beautiful—and muggy and buggy. There are five different climate zones that you move through when climbing up Mount Kilimanjaro, which adds to the uniqueness of the journey. Although our first campsite was in the tropical rainforest, we also traveled through the alpine desert and the arctic zone. It's been said that climbing Kilimanjaro is like traveling from the equator to the North Pole. We dressed in layers as the weather was at times unpredictable.

Our leader, Chris Warner, author of *High Altitude Leadership*, was far more than just our leader—he was our mentor. He has led over two hundred international expeditions. He was the ninth American to have summited both K2 and Mount Everest. He emphasized that we were much stronger as a team than as individuals—and that teams are built on trust and caring.

Working together as a team really lightened the burden. If one person was struggling with the weight of their pack, we would distribute their belongings, each of us carrying slightly more for somebody else, depending on how people felt that day. Everything we did was a team effort.

The climb was difficult. The lack of oxygen and the extreme altitude was taxing. But one of the most challenging parts for me about the whole experience was the absence of creature comforts, especially the luxury of a toilet with flushing water. I felt like I had to go to the bathroom all the time, including at 2:00 a.m., 3:00 a.m., and 4:00 a.m. I would have to psyche myself up to peel back the warmth of my sleeping bag, unzip the tent, and slide on my shoes. I had four layers of clothes on, but I was still freezing. The idea of having to take all of my layers off every time I had to pee was overwhelming. Fortunately I had planned for the intricacies of peeing in the woods. Before I left for the trip, I purchased a pee funnel for $19.99. It allowed me to pee standing up. Best purchase ever! Other women on the trip were both inquisitive and jealous of this tool. I'm typically a sharer, but not in this case. Thankfully, this small and simple tool made my life just a little bit easier.

When the life that you're used to is no longer right in front of you, you have to decide how you're going to react. It would be so easy to complain about the things we no longer had. But in general, I think everybody realized we were all there for the same reason. We were raising money for the Livestrong Foundation, and we were doing something really cool together. By remembering our "why," we were able to accomplish the seemingly impossible.

### YOU SHOULD NEVER WALK YOUR JOURNEY ALONE

I was fortunate to have the best tent mate, Ronda. We got along from the second we met. With Ronda's help I learned how to properly use a sleeping bag—the drawstring makes the difference between freezing and warmth. We also shared some of the funniest moments of the hike together. For example, one night we awoke to one of the guys in the next tent screaming that someone had stolen his purse. We heard his wife, who was sharing the tent with him, respond back, "Seriously, someone stole your purse?" We couldn't stop laughing. Anti-malarial meds offer up some crazy dreams.

Having Ronda as my partner made the climb much easier to travel. Probably the most valuable lesson I learned is that our journey isn't just about us. There are people all around ready and willing to help us when the mountain gets harder to climb. We are never alone, but we must allow people in to help us, and we must be willing to help other people.

We were only allowed a certain amount of weight that we could carry in our packs while we were inside the national park, so strong, fast porters helped us all along the way, carrying some of our bags and our tents. They would wait for us to depart the camp, pack up all of the tents and supplies, pass us on the trail en route to the next camp, and have the entire camp set back up again before we arrived.

By the time we reached the camp at night, they had popcorn and hot water waiting for us. They would then proceed to serve us a delicious gourmet meal. It was unbelievable what they could prepare on the mountain. I was continuously amazed by what the porters were able to do.

For the last part of the ascent, I was partnered with my new friend, Mike. He would have stood out even if he hadn't been my partner because he had the most energy and the best attitude of anyone I've ever met. Although younger than many in the group, Mike had lived a lifetime of experience in his short life. After being diagnosed with acute myeloid leukemia at the age of ten, Mike would eventually endure two bone marrow transplants and more than seventy-five surgeries. One surgery included the removal of a bone cancer tumor and more than half of his lower jaw, and then replacing it with the fibula from his left leg.

He was one of the most positive people I'd ever met. He was an everyday hero and the most inspirational person for me on the trip. No matter what difficulty we were facing, his answer was always the same: "You can do this."

Those words weren't just Mike trying to motivate us to keep moving; he knew the truth behind those words. We could tell that he meant what he said, and his sincerity made his words even more motivating. I generally don't doubt myself in challenging situations, and with Mike around, any doubt I might have had, dissolved. His positivity and motivation kept all of us moving forward.

Life often gives us unique opportunities to make choices that, in the moment, seem small. Looking back on our journey, we get to see how each choice leads us to something greater. For me, the choice to climb Mount Kilimanjaro was one of those choices. Because of that simple choice, I got to meet people I never would've met otherwise. And together we climbed Africa's tallest mountain. My life has been forever impacted by the people on this journey.

## REACHING THE SUMMIT

One day we were walking and one of the guys in our group had Michael Jackson playing on his wireless speaker. He was successfully doing the moonwalk as we walked the trail. Our leader, Chris Warner, kept saying, "Don't waste your pennies; you can't get them back." Chris was so right. Later, that same guy was exhausted because when you expend that much energy, it's really hard to recoup at high altitude. That was a valuable lesson as we got into even higher altitudes.

The summit attempt would take us from 15,420 feet to 19,341 feet. We began our ascent at 11:00 p.m. on the fifth night and hiked through the darkness. I can still picture it in my mind. The trail was pitch black; we had only our headlamps to guide us and the lights of those in front of us. We followed the trail as it curved back and forth in switchbacks all the way up the mountain. Rhythmically we walked together, each small step taking us farther up the mountain.

Several people began struggling as we got closer to the top because of the altitude that we were reaching. The higher we climbed, the less oxygen there was. We were walking very slowly because it was a struggle for each of us to even get our body to walk at all. At this point, it doesn't matter how hard you've trained—your body has to adjust to the oxygen-deprived conditions of high altitude.

I could see splatters of blood on the trail, most likely from hikers who were suffering from bloody noses caused by the altitude. We were pushing our bodies to the limits, and it was definitely a test of our determination and our physical and mental strength. But each of us was driven to make it to the top of the mountain.

## THE VALUE OF TEAMWORK

Before we even started trekking up the mountain, we had to make the decision to work as a team. And once we made that decision, there was no going back.

When one person in the group was having difficulty, we had to ask the hard questions like: "Are we going to the top together?" or "If one person can't make it, what are the rest of us going to do?" These questions were important to the welfare of everyone. As a team, we had to decide how we were going to move forward. The real question was, "Do we stay back?"

One team member started getting a terrible cough before we even began the final ascent. She couldn't control it, but she was a marathon runner and wouldn't give up. She insisted that we all keep moving at our normal pace, and she would keep moving at her pace. The main concern with everyone slowing down was that other people were also struggling with the altitude. We needed to keep moving forward to get them to the top before they sat too long in the thin air. There was only so much time that people could handle the low oxygen levels at high altitude.

One of the younger members of our group was very athletic, and he volunteered to stay back with her to ensure that she wouldn't be alone. He didn't even hesitate. One of the guides and a couple of the porters walked with them, while the rest of us made our way ahead of them to the top of the mountain.

This remarkable woman never gave up, and we all made it to the top. Although my brain may have been a little fuzzy from the lack of oxygen, I will never forget the feeling I had summiting that mountain with my team.

That's the beauty of working on a team and doing things together. We can lean on one another in our times of trouble and still make it to our destination. We can also learn so much from one another. And often what we see as our final destination is just another leg of the journey.

## YOU DON'T HAVE TO MOVE MOUNTAINS, BUT YOU STILL HAVE TO CLIMB THEM

When I think of my friend, Mike, I'm inspired by his ability to endure everything life has thrown at him, and to still help others along the way. His journey reminds all of us that there will be times in our life when we have to face figurative mountains. And the only way to conquer them is to climb.

Mike was, and still is, the perfect example of someone who has faced figurative mountains much larger than Mount Kilimanjaro. Because of his courage to climb, he has come out on top every single time. Perhaps the most astounding thing about his journey is that he has lived it with purpose and passion. While everyone was walking slowly up the mountain, Mike was jumping on rocks, like it was no big deal. He obviously had a lot of pennies to spare. His energy was contagious, and certainly worth catching. But the thing that inspired me the most about Mike is that he had been through so much in his life, and yet he always saw the good.

Obstacles are going to be a part of every journey; it's how we deal with the obstacles that really matters and makes a difference. They often come when we least expect them, and they feel gigantic and overwhelming. Sometimes we can move around them, but most of the time we have to climb over them. Rather than sit down and give up, we can choose to face them head-on and start climbing.

The perspective of that mountain looks much different from the top. I remember being at the summit of Mount Kilimanjaro and feeling an overwhelming sense of gratitude in my heart as I raised my flag dedicated to cancer survivors and those who lost their battle. Some of our greatest moments will be from the top of our mountains looking back down our path. Because from that perspective, we gain confidence in ourselves as we see just how far we've come. Everything is breathtaking from the top, and the only way to see that spectacular view is to climb.

But sometimes, the figurative mountains we face aren't really mountains at all. Have you ever heard the phrase "making mountains out of molehills"? Sometimes we get so focused on something that it clouds our view and we can't see beyond it—just like focusing on my thumb made it so I couldn't see Mount Kilimanjaro. Sometimes, stepping back and looking at the big picture allows us to put those figurative mountains in their proper perspective.

So many times, we get caught up in the little things—things that don't really matter. Sometimes we look at obstacles in front of us, and we see them as so great that we don't want to move forward. But if we change the way we look at it, our mountain really can be more like a molehill. Sometimes.

But whether your obstacle is a mountain or a molehill, this

same principle applies—both are conquered one step at a time.

## YOU CLIMB A MOUNTAIN ONE SMALL STEP AT A TIME

Mount Kilimanjaro was certainly not a molehill. Even though it looked as if I could pinch it between my fingers when we were far away, close up it was definitely an obstacle. The only way to the top was one step at a time.

I believe that's the only way you can face anything—head-on, one foot in front of the other. Any challenge we have, or obstacle we face, can only be conquered one small step after another, until we reach the summit.

Sometimes we have challenges that seem insurmountable—an impossible challenge with impossible odds against us. But nothing is impossible. If you break it down to one step at a time, things no longer seem overwhelming.

As we climbed Mount Kilimanjaro, our leader encouraged us to concentrate on walking heel to toe, heel to toe, in small even steps. In his words, "we were preserving and reserving energy for when we needed it most." With slow and steady movements, we focused on what we needed to do in that moment, and nothing more. There were times when we had thousands of steps to take up the mountain before we reached our next camp. The thought alone could have been overwhelming if we considered it all at once. To progress in our journey, we couldn't think about what was coming or what more we had to do; we simply put one foot in front of the other. We found that we took the most steps when we really focused on taking just one step at a time.

If you're looking at your journey as just one step at a time, you don't really think about how long it is going to take you to get to where you are going. Instead, you find joy in the journey, and the journey becomes the destination. With each step you take, you think to yourself, "Okay, one more step. I can do this!"

## WE ARE MUCH STRONGER TOGETHER

It's hard to believe that climbing a mountain can impact your life so deeply and change your mind on things. But it was truly life-changing not only to climb Mount Kilimanjaro, but to climb it together.

It was the support of a team that made climbing Mount Kilimanjaro possible. Without the team, it would have been even more challenging to make it to the top. It was an experience that helped me to recognize the impact we can have when we walk our journeys together. And when we walk together, we have the capacity to do so much good.

We should never feel like we have to walk our journey

alone. Walking with people who support us adds to our own strength and makes us much more effective in everything that we do. Our overall journey will be better and the lasting effects of it more powerful because we're sharing that experience with someone else. When we truly connect with others, their love and energy helps us to accomplish so much more.

I truly believe life is just like climbing a mountain. We need each other. Just like on the mountain, when we have a team around us that supports us, everything becomes much easier, and the impossible journey becomes possible.

My team was my strength as I climbed up Mount Kilimanjaro. But it is my home team who gives me my greatest strength. It is my husband and my children who cheer me on and encourage me to keep moving forward.

While I was climbing Mount Kilimanjaro, we reached the first summit at 5:00 a.m., right as the sun was rising. It was a breathtaking view and glorious to behold. When I took my phone out to take a picture of the scene, so that I could share it with my family when I returned home, I realized that I had cell service—something that was rare on the trip.

I immediately called home, and instead of sharing that moment in a picture, I was able to share it with them in real time and describe exactly what I was seeing. They shared in my excitement, and it was as if they were right there with me. Even after we hung up, I carried them with me every step of the way.

I couldn't have accomplished any of the things I've been able to do without the support and strength of my family. Together we're strong. We help carry one another. When times are tough we're there for each other. When times are great, we celebrate!

I was able to climb Mount Kilimanjaro because back home I had a team who made it possible. My husband cared for the kids, and the kids made sacrifices so that I could do it. While climbing Mount Kilimanjaro may seem like a great accomplishment, my greatest accomplishment is being a mother to six pretty remarkable kids. They are my people.

Everyone needs people they can turn to for support. Be that person for others, and find those people for yourself. I'm so lucky I've found those people in my husband and children. It's not always easy letting others in—but it will always be worth it.

Climbing Mount Kilimanjaro was a once-in-a-lifetime adventure. But the lessons that I brought down from that mountain have changed my life forever. Every journey is taken one step at a time, and there is strength in walking with others. But one of the greatest lessons I learned, while walking up that mountain one small step at a time and working with a team of strangers along the way, is that patience is key in all of it.

# Chapter 9

# LIFE ISN'T ALWAYS FAIR

## THINGS WE CANNOT CHANGE

As I sat next to Olivia, waiting for her to wake up from her colonoscopy, all I could think of was, "Please let her be okay."

Olivia's eyes began to open, and she smiled as she whispered, "You're here." Her eyes closed, she slept for another fifteen minutes, and then again opened her eyes, looked at me, and smiled. "You're here," she said. Her eyes closed again. I was so tempted to take a video of her next eye-opening experience, but I decided that it would be a "bad" parenting moment. Boy, do I regret that decision.

The gastroenterologist walked up to her bedside. "First of all," he said, "I know you were really worried that she may have cancer, but she does not."

I breathed a huge sigh of relief.

"But," he said, "she has Crohn's. It's really serious. And so, I need you to take it very seriously. I know she can't really understand what we're talking about—obviously the anesthesia did its job—but I need you to understand the seriousness of this." He then showed me the pictures of her small bowel, which had ulcers all over it. We could definitely tell from the photos just how sick she really was. "It's really bad right now," he said. "And although it will get better, this is something she's going to live with forever."

He then continued to outline everything that came with it, and I started crying inside. This is the girl who loves ethnic food, plans her day around soup, and intends on sampling her way around the world. I was trying to stay strong on the outside for Olivia, even though she was still under the effects of the anesthesia and would remember nothing from the conversation. But inside, I was a complete wreck. She was only sixteen years old, and she had her whole life ahead of her. It just wasn't fair.

Leading up to the diagnosis, Olivia had been struggling for years with stomach problems. At first, we thought that maybe she was lactose intolerant, so she stopped eating dairy. Then we thought maybe she had Celiac, so she started eating gluten-free. She was really watching what she ate, but over the course of the three months before the actual diagnosis, she started losing a lot of weight and was starting to look pale and sickly.

I joke with others who have children that with child number one, you sanitize everything and run to the doctor over a nose sniffle. Child number two, if something falls on the floor, you implement the five-second rule. Child number three, you pull it out of the garbage, and it's still good. Child four, five, and six, anything goes. By the time you get to that point, it really doesn't matter anymore. You realize that germs happen, no matter what your sanitization procedure is. Because we have six kids, we tend not to react as quickly to things like a stomachache. We get a lot of stomachaches at our house, and most of them don't amount to anything. That's just the reality of things. We have so much going on at any given moment that we have to prioritize. Of course, looking back, we still feel guilty that we waited for so long. Parent guilt is a real thing.

When Olivia was finally awake, or at least awake enough to comprehend basic words, we discussed her diagnosis and all of things she needed to do moving forward. The only thing she heard me say was that she had to stay on a liquid diet for another two days. The sky had fallen.

As she was prepping for her colonoscopy and attempting to drink the nastiest of liquids that were to empty her bowels, the only thing that helped her swallow the vile substance was the notion that she could have an amazing meal, complete with Thai food from her favorite takeout spot, post-colonoscopy. The prep was so bad for her that I literally had to draw lines with a sharpie on her cup so that she could have goals. Three sips to line number one, six sips to line number two, one last gulp, and she was done. With all of this hard work behind her and the colonoscopy done, she was devastated that she would be required to consume only liquids for two more days. In the moment, I honestly think she was more upset about the inability to have a meal versus her actual diagnosis.

The extreme and strict diet that the doctor recommended for her to begin after the two days of liquid was the hardest thing for her to process. He recommended that she stick to a low-fiber diet for a few weeks to help her gut calm down. We called it the white-trash diet because basically everything that was okay to eat went against all healthy rationale—and it was all white. Her menu included white rice, mashed potatoes, and white bread. It was a real struggle for her to imagine a life without the foods she loved. What's more, her diagnosis came right before Thanksgiving. The idea of spending a holiday that is all about food and family, without the ability to actually eat the food, was a hard thing to accept—so we changed the menu. We had a white trash Thanksgiving in her honor.

As a mom, watching my sixteen-year-old daughter go through this difficult diagnosis wasn't easy. All I could do was help her through it with words of comfort, support, and humor.

"This is just for right now," I said. "And when you get through this part, then we'll figure out what the next part is. You can't look at it like you're going to have to do this for the next seventy years. For now, we're going to get through the next two days on a liquid diet. And then we're going to focus on the low-fiber diet to get things to calm down. After that, we'll figure out what works and what comes next. We're going to take it one small chunk at a time. Don't look at it and think, 'My life is over: I can never travel, I can never go anywhere fun, I can never eat this kind of food again.' We're just living it one day at a time. So, let's focus on what we can do today to make it better."

But what I said inside my mind was: "I've waited all my life for a doctor to tell me to eat mashed potatoes and white rice. Embrace it!" For me, humor always helps to make trials a little more bearable.

When we're faced with hard things, it's so easy to go down a path of misery. But there's nothing good there. Olivia's first reaction when she was told she would have to go on steroids for a couple of months was, "I'm going to get really fat and my face is going to be covered in pimples."

It's human nature to see the bad in our situation before we

see the good. But focusing on the bad is not going to help us get through the situation. It's just going to make us more miserable as we're going through it. The best thing we can do for ourselves is acknowledge the hard in life without letting it stop us from progressing.

We sat on the couch, turned our phones on do-not-disturb, cried some tears, and then reminded ourselves of all of the good things that are possible. We're moving forward one day at a time, accepting the things we cannot change, and trying to improve the things we can.

Our family attitude is, "Life isn't always fair, but it is what it is. So, let's figure out how to make the best of what we have in front of us." This is how we try to face every difficult thing life throws at us. But that doesn't mean that we don't have our moments of tears and frustration too.

## IT'S OKAY TO CRY WHEN THINGS GET HARD

Because we're all human, I don't think there's a person in this world who is truly happy all of the time. If they are, they're misrepresenting themselves and their life. Everyone will have moments in their lives when they will become frustrated, upset, or disappointed. In those moments of pain and sadness, it's important to allow ourselves to feel the pain and sorrow. That is the only way we will be able to get through to the other side of it.

I consider myself a pretty positive person. But even I have moments of anger and frustration. When we were sitting in the doctor's office and he was outlining everything Olivia would have to do, I started thinking, "This sucks! This is something she has to deal with forever. It's not like she has an infection and she's going to take some antibiotics and it's going to be done. This is a forever thing, and this is so not fair!" I allowed myself to feel the anger, the sorrow for her future, and the pain that comes from knowing I couldn't fix it.

When those unfair things happen, give yourself the time to be upset. Give yourself time to be angry. Because if you don't, you're going to spend the rest of your life masking it because you've stuffed it down and never really faced it and dealt with the emotion. But once you allow yourself time to grieve, move your journey forward.

After I felt all of the emotions that came with Olivia's diagnosis, I had to move on, especially for Olivia's sake. I realized that there are so many worse things that Olivia could have. She was going to get through this, and as a family, we were going to help her.

For Olivia, it was important that I also gave her time to grieve. I told her, "Be angry! Be mad! Be sad! But pick a day, and tell yourself that on that day, you're not going to be upset anymore and let it go." I encouraged her to choose a day that was not too far away, because keeping those emotions for an extended period of time is never a good idea.

"Okay," she said, "let me just be miserable until Sunday, and on Sunday I'll regroup."

"Okay," I said, "that's fair. You get time to be miserable about it, and then we create the plan on how to move forward."

I encouraged her to say to herself, "I'm going to feel sorry for myself, especially because I can't eat real food. I'm going to cry if I want to. I'm going to be angry and I don't want to talk to my friends this weekend. I just want to bury my head in a hole and cry it out. Then on Sunday, I'm going to remind myself that this was the day I decided to start moving forward. And that's what I'm going to do."

And because of the remarkable human she is, that is exactly what she did.

It's a part of the human experience to feel those emotions when they come. But we can't sit in those emotions forever—we need to keep moving forward. That is the key. Allow yourself time to grieve, and then move on from them. That is how we get through those hard, unfair times.

The reality of life is that we're going to have some really tough times, and we will face things that seem completely unfair. But we have to learn how to move forward anyway. No matter who you are, those hard days are going to come to you, because they are a part of everyone's journey. You may react to that day by lying down on the floor and crying about it. But eventually, you have to realize that lying on the floor and crying about it is doing you no good. Choose to get up, wipe away your tears, and make a plan on how you're going to move forward. Part of our journey is learning how to move through those unfair things so we can learn from them and keep progressing in our journey.

## ROSE-COLORED GLASSES

There are so many fears that come when you find yourself in circumstances that force you to change your everyday life. One of Olivia's fears was that she would go to school and, as she became more and more swollen from the steroids, the kids would start making fun of her.

My encouragement to her was that she should educate people on the disease so that they could have a better understanding of what she was going through. I truly believe that most of the judgments that come from people happen because they don't know what they're talking about. It's true that some people are mean, but most people just don't understand the situation. That's why we can really add value to the world if we share our experiences and use them to help educate others.

Olivia's diagnosis came at the same time she was writing essays for her college applications. The day after she got the diagnosis, this is the essay she wrote:

"Frank Sinatra once sang, 'I'm lookin' at the world through rose-colored glasses, everything is rosy now.' Although wearing rose-colored glasses would, in fact, change the color of everything around you to a rosy tint, that's probably not what Sinatra meant. To see the world through rose-colored glasses is to choose to see the world for the best it could be. It's common knowledge that there is not a manual on how to live life. It's a game of educated guessing with frequent stops at points that seem impossible to pass through. During these pauses, it's sometimes necessary to see the world through rose-colored glasses in order to overcome obstacles. To many, this may come off as hiding from how bad things truly are; these people argue that constant positivity leads to an unrealistic view of the world. I reject that notion. Sometimes the only way to survive life's hardships is to view them through a lens of positivity.

Although I am only sixteen years old, I have definitely experienced moments in which rose-colored glasses were needed. One of these moments came yesterday when I was diagnosed with severe Crohn's disease. While the doctor was explaining what that means, all I could think about was how this would alter my future. How will this affect my plans for college, careers, or even family? When my mom and I finally left the hospital, I started sobbing. I couldn't think of a way to manage this life-changing burden. How can I solve an issue when there is no means of actually fixing it? How can I come to terms with a hardship that will never go away? Everyone, at some point in their lives, will have a moment like this, where the task at hand seems next to impossible. To look at these situations through rose-colored glasses is to wrest power from a situation that seeks to rob you of it. To refuse to let it define the rest of your life is an act of courage, not cowardice.

As I write this essay, I am trying my best to see this diagnosis through rose-colored glasses. After months of pain and uncertainty, I finally have a clear answer, although it comes with a cloudy solution. To be honest, I am struggling to find the energy to view the situation with optimism. However, I am hopeful that I will be able to find the positivity needed to persist. While I don't know how my path may end, it seems to me that hiding from reality behind Sinatra's rosy shades is not so bad after all, at least for now."

When our path takes us into difficult terrain, we have two choices. We can let it break us, or we can let it bolster us. I have learned a great deal from my sixteen-year-old daughter through this experience. We both tend to see the world through rose-colored glasses, and I think that's exactly as it should be. What truly defines our journey is how we move forward when life isn't easy.

## SOME DAYS YOU WON'T FEEL LIKE ADULTING

Even if you haven't been hit with some heavy, life-changing news, there are going to be days you won't feel like adulting. Believe me when I say that I've had my fair share of these days.

I've had horrible insomnia for the last couple of years. I'm not sure why it started; all I know is that it seems to be here to stay. When I do sleep, I tend to have crazy, vivid dreams. One night recently, when I finally fell asleep, I started having this crazy dream where Noah was screaming my name. It felt so real that I opened my eyes and shot up in bed. It was 1:41 a.m. As I sat there, I listened carefully but didn't hear a thing. I convinced myself that it was only a dream. I figured that since I was already awake, I would go to the bathroom and get a drink of water, otherwise it was a totally wasted wake-up. On my way back to bed, I decided to do a quick walk-through of the house, because that's what insomniacs do.

Noah may not have screamed my name, but I found him wide awake sitting in front of the TV at nearly 2:00 a.m. "Noah," I said, "are you kidding me?! I don't want to adult right now. It's two o'clock in the morning, which means it's also the middle of the night! Why are you down here? You know the rules. Even if you wake up or you can't fall asleep, you have to stay in your room."

"I'm not tired," he said.

"Well, I'm really tired. Go to bed!"

Arguing with my child about the importance of sleep was not what I wanted to do in the middle of the night. What I wanted to do was walk through the house, get my glass of water, and go back to bed. But sometimes life gets in the way of the best-laid plans.

As a kid I couldn't wait to become an adult. Adults got to make their own choices. They got to vote, they were allowed to drink alcohol, and they could even own a house. But the things I failed to understand were the responsibilities that came along with adulting. I didn't get that memo. To whom much is given, much is expected.

Often, as adults, we're placed in situations that force us into doing things that we would otherwise not want to do, because of the responsibilities that we have taken upon ourselves. That's part of being a responsible adult—being able to deal with the things that come our way.

**MAMA SAID THERE WILL BE DAYS LIKE THIS**

There are going to be times in life when, instead of getting out of bed, we want to pull the covers over our head and sleep the whole day through. There are going to be days when facing that day seems difficult and overwhelming, but we have to face it anyway.

There will be days when I wake up and say to the kids, "I don't feel like adulting today. Can we just watch a movie? Have breakfast for dinner?" Or even better, "Cook for me, please?" Thankfully, my kids get it. A lot of times they don't feel like doing things either. They will happily join in on a movie marathon while eating pancakes. Some days are just going to be like that.

I don't think there's one adult who feels like they want to be responsible 100 percent of the time. And sometimes, as a mother, each new day is a never-ending cycle of cooking, cleaning, chauffeuring, and refereeing, in addition to a thousand other things. You never know from day to day what's going to hit you.

When those days come when I really don't feel like I can pack one more lunch, or referee one more battle, the best thing for everyone involved is to have my kids do the adulting for me. I know it sounds like bad parenting, but it actually works quite well.

For example, there was a period of time when Noah really struggled to get dressed in the morning. He would just lie on the couch, and I would say to him, "Noah, get your shirt on." Then he'd get a shirt on. Then I would say, "Noah, get your shorts on." Then he would get his shorts on. And I would have to continue this back-and-forth until he put on every article of clothing—every single day, of every single week, of every single year. Finally, one day it came down to him getting his socks on and he wouldn't do it. I thought to myself, "Oh my gosh, am I going to do this until he's forty?"

Mili saw the struggle and my frustration and stepped in. "It's okay, Mom," she said. "I got it today."

I loved that she thought she could fix what I had been working on for years. I was so curious to see how she was going to handle him. She walked to where he was lying on the couch. "Hi, baby," she said.

"Who are you talking to?" Noah asked.

"I'm talking to you," she said back to him.

"I'm not a baby," Noah said.

"Well, you must be," Mili said, "because only babies can't put their socks on."

That's all it took. Noah immediately put his socks on, and I never had another problem with getting him to do it.

While her approach was less than traditional, it was exactly the push Noah needed to take responsibility for dressing himself, and it made our mornings so much easier.

Some battles can only be won when we look at them differently. Mili saw my frustrations as a challenge, and she used a completely different approach to a battle I had been fighting for years. From this experience I learned that I'll never win the battle if I always do what I've always done. She reminded me that the definition of insanity was doing the same thing over and over again and expecting a different result.

Adulting doesn't mean that we always have to see things through grown-up eyes. Sometimes, our problems can be solved by letting go of our adult expectations and seeing the situation from a very different perspective. As adults, we sometimes make things more difficult than they have to be. On the days you don't feel like adulting, try to simplify your expectations and allow yourself to do things differently. Remind yourself that it's okay.

## LISTEN, BUT DON'T ENABLE

As a mom, I know that everyone needs to voice their concerns to a listening ear. You should hear our dinner table. The kids talk so much that they eventually start raising their hand and get put into a queue. We've even created a written list of who gets to speak next. Their voices must be heard, but sometimes the entire discussion takes a negative turn and the whole table starts airing their concerns and complaints for the day.

Misery loves company, and when someone is feeling miserable, they start looking for others who will be miserable with them. That's just how we work as humans. We don't want to be alone, even in our misery.

When Olivia was diagnosed with Crohn's disease, it would have been so easy for me to become an enabler as she talked about how her life would never be the same. And while she was right, her life would never be the same, constantly reminding her of that, or agreeing with her every time she said it, would not have been helpful.

I could have said to her, "Oh, this is horrible. It's just going to be so stressful. I don't think you can go away to college. I think you should go to the local community college." I could have told her everything I was thinking and feeling. But it would have pushed her into even deeper sorrow.

Instead, I said, "Yes, we're going to have all of these things to think about and it's going to be on a daily basis. It's important that we make choices every day that will make sure you're in the place you need to be. But you don't have to do this alone. I am here to help you. We'll do it together."

Was I angry about her diagnosis? Absolutely. Was I sad that her life from that moment on was going to change drastically? Of course, I was. But I was not going to just give up and let my fears and emotions lead me. My job as her mom was, and still is, to figure out how to help her move forward and to make sure she can have the best life she can possibly have. Just sitting there feeling sorry about the circumstances wasn't going to make a difference in her life. Being compassionate toward her and listening to her very valid concerns was absolutely necessary. But joining her in her misery by voicing my own sadness about her situation would have amounted to both of us struggling to pick ourselves back up again. I simply acknowledged that she was right and moved on to create a plan to help her move forward in her new circumstances.

When someone comes to you with their sadness, listen to them and comfort them, but don't let them stay there in their misery for too long. They need to experience those emotions, but they also need to move on from them. Remind them that there are answers, that there are brighter days ahead, and there's always help to be found. Try not to let their negative emotions rub off on you.

Some of the greatest good you can do in your journey is to support others when their journey gets tough and help them find the way out of their own despair.

## WE ALL NEED A PERSON

When we are in that place of sadness, it's important that we have that person in our life who can help pull us out of it.

Our journey is made easier when we have someone whom we can reach out to when the days get hard. After we've cried about the curveball life has thrown at us, our person is the one who will help to build us back up again. We all need that person.

When you say, "Today really sucks. It is the worst day, ever," your person needs to be the kind of person who responds with, "You know what? It really does suck, but tomorrow is going to be better," versus, "You're right, it really does suck, and it's going to suck from now on. I don't know why you bother."

You need that person who will listen to you, cry with you when your date didn't go well, and then, at the appropriate moment, tell you, "Okay, you're done crying about this; move forward. He wasn't good enough for you anyway." That's who your person is—the one who will listen to you whine and cry, and also the one who will tell you when it's time to stop crying and move forward.

I think it's important to have someone who, when you call, will answer and will be brutally honest with you. They'll tell you what you need to hear, not necessarily what you want to hear: "Pick a different outfit; it's not flattering." "It's time to dye your hair; your grays are popping." "Don't go out with your ex; you know how it's going to end up." You need someone who will be genuine and true, even when there are hard things to be said.

Whether your person is a family member or a friend, make sure you have that person you can lean on when you find it hard to stand on your own. We all need that person to help direct us when we've lost our direction, to strengthen us when we've lost our strength, and to tell us exactly what we need to hear.

We often wait for the storms of life to pass so we can enjoy the sunshine. But as a mother, one thing I've noticed is that kids aren't that way. Like Olivia, they see the world through rose-colored glasses. When the storms come, they put on their boots and raincoats and go dance in the puddles. We aren't meant to be at the mercy of life's weather. We're meant to make our own rainbows and share them with everyone around us.

*Chapter 10*

# THE WORLD AS I SEE IT

## UNDERSTANDING DIVERSITY

There are nearly eight billion people in the world, and each one of us is different. We have different beliefs, different characteristics, different hopes and dreams, different jobs, different houses, and different families. We are extremely diverse—and that is a really good thing.

Diversity is our world. We might often think of diversity as color, or maybe even religion. But it's much more than that. Diversity doesn't just mean color, and it doesn't just mean religion. It means people. It's the ability to understand that people are going to be different than you, and to respect them for that. Whether it's someone who thinks differently than you, someone from a different culture or religious background, someone who has a unique story, or someone who speaks a different language—it's all part of diversity.

When discussing diversity with Emma, she said it best: "Diversity is the ability for everyone to be who they are without being judged for it." It really should be that simple.

I believe the problem that the world has, in general, is that we judge people before we even know them. We make assumptions about people based on the first thing we see, which has very little to do with what actually is. For example, people see Noah, and because he's Asian, they assume he loves dumplings and fried rice. It's a ridiculous assumption, but I hear it all the time. The reality is that he is the pickiest eater on the planet and won't eat any of those foods. Another example is people see that I have six kids, and they automatically assume that I'm ultra-religious, even though they know nothing about me. But I'm not—I'm a human just trying to do my part.

## DIFFERENCES ARE ESSENTIAL

As I see the current state of our world, there are so many things I wish I could change. For example, I'm not a black mother, and I could never begin to understand what black mothers go through while raising their kids. But I am a mother of black children. I am and forever will be disheartened that my children have been and will be treated differently because of the color of their skin. I've had to have conversations with Ari that I never had to have with Jacob: "Keep your hands on the steering wheel if you're ever pulled over by a police officer." "Don't walk around the neighborhood by yourself at night." "Don't put your hoodie up unless we're around." It's heartbreaking to see and it's never okay.

Ari got his boating license last summer. The first day Ari took the jet ski out by himself he got pulled over. When I asked him why, he said, "Because I'm black. Look around mom...How many black people do you see on a jet ski in Sarasota?" He said the officer not only asked to see his boating license and his ID, but he insisted that Ari point out what house he lived in. The police officer wrote him a warning for going too fast in a no-wake zone. Yet it wasn't even a no-wake zone. It's tragic that Ari has to do things differently than his white brother because we live in a world where people make false assumptions based on what others looks like, and then they immediately act on those assumptions.

I want to help people understand that differences are essential. They are what make the world a really great place to be. It all depends on how we see things. Just like we can choose whether to be miserable or happy, we get to choose how we look at the world around us, and the kind of person we are going to be. If we walk into a room and choose to look at the people in it with dignity and respect, imagine the good we could do for so many, simply by seeing them as the unique people that they are.

## THE CHANGE THE WORLD NEEDS

We recently had a repairman visit our house to complete some work. He was a very nice man and was very helpful. He started talking about current events and brought up NASCAR's decision to prohibit displaying Confederate flags at all NASCAR events and properties. He was angry and proceeded to tell me how angry his friends were about it because they believe that the flag is just a piece of United States history.

As soon as he started talking about it, I felt a pit in my stomach. I knew he wanted me to agree with him. I wanted to be angry at him for being insensitive and closed-minded. But I realized that this was the perfect opportunity to make a positive difference, or at least share my own beliefs in a respectful way. Rather than choose anger, I asked him how he felt about the Nazi flag. Would he support people who wanted to display that flag?

Honestly, his answer could have gone in either direction with that question. Fortunately, however, he said, "Of course not. The Nazis killed millions of people."

"Well, the Nazi flag is also a piece of history," I responded.

"It reminds us that we cannot stay silent when it comes to the unjust persecution and destruction of humans. I would not go near a place that flew the Nazi flag. Yes, the Confederate flag is a piece of history, but it represents a horrible part of our history. It's an artifact that makes tangible the truth of the past, a historic relic that depicts a time period when millions of people died because of the slave trade, a reminder of the inhumane treatment of black people, and a failure of humanity. To me, the Confederate flag is not something to be displayed with pride. I see it as a reminder of how much further we still need to go."

He looked at me, nodded his head up and down, and said, "I never thought about it like that before. I really only thought about it as a piece of United States history."

What he did with that conversation, I will probably never know. I would like to believe that I at least got him to think beyond what he thought he knew. For me, I was reminded of the importance of using my words and not remaining silent—even when I'm uncomfortable and the conversation is challenging.

As I move forward on my journey, I understand that I have a lot to learn. I need to listen without ego and defensiveness because I cannot pretend to understand or know what anyone else is going through.

Many people fear using the wrong words, or they are scared of saying the wrong things—trying to show support for black lives but unsure of how to express themselves. We must realize that we have to get over the fear of making mistakes and get out of our comfort zone. I am not an activist, nor have I ever pretended to be. But I believe that everyone should be treated with respect.

I used to tell myself to pick my battles because some people will never change. But we must not stay silent. We can't just tiptoe. If we are going to contribute to this process of necessary change, then we are going to feel discomfort. Justice is critical and extremely important, but it is inadequate for the lives lost.

What the world needs is fairness and equality for all. People need to understand that every individual is integral to the fabric of society. I have children from three different nationalities, and they are all precious to me.

In this day and age, anger needs to become unity. Destruction needs to become bridge building. And most importantly, we must move forward with love and understanding.

Maya Angelou said, "We all should know that diversity makes for rich tapestry, and we must understand that all of the threads of the tapestry are equal in value no matter what their color." For me, it even goes beyond that, though.

We're equal in value no matter our color, our shape, our size, our beliefs, our family, and the list goes on and on. We all matter, and we all have the capacity for kindness and respect. When we talk about making a difference in the world, embracing diversity and seeing everyone as uniquely beautiful and completely valued is one of the greatest differences we can make.

I see our world as diverse, and it's the acceptance of that diversity that's so important to me. It's not about pointing out how we're different—it's about realizing that, despite our differences, our value is always the same.

## THE SEVEN JEWISH VALUES I LIVE BY

Maybe I see the world differently because of the pieces of Judaism that are most important to me, like the Seven Jewish Values of an inclusive community.

These are the values I grew up with, and the values that I have passed down to my own children. It's not just about religion; it's about being the good in the world, and being the good for the world. These values have helped to define my journey.

*Kavod* (**Respect**): *Kavod* is about treating ourselves and others with respect, including strangers. It is regarding the rights, dignity, and feelings of others, and respecting and valuing people's differences, rather than ostracizing them and judging them because of those differences.

**Shalom Bayit (Peace in the Home):** *Shalom Bayit* reminds us that we all need to have a safe space where we feel comfortable and respected. It is about learning how to settle disagreements respectfully and with dignity. This idea goes beyond our own homes and drives how we treat one another in our synagogues and other community events.

**B'tzelem Elohim (In God's Image):** We are taught that we are all in the image of God, which guides how we treat others. If we see the image of God in others, we can see the good and the humanity in all people.

**Kol Yisrael Arevim Zeh Bazeh (Communal Responsibility):** This literally translates to "All Israel is responsible for one another." This means that we have the responsibility to take action to make the world a better place, and that we also have the responsibility to inspire others to take positive actions as well.

**Sh'mirat Halashon (Guarding One's Use of Language):** In the Jewish community, we learn that our words matter. They can hurt others, or they can heal, depending on what words we use. Speaking about others behind their backs can be damaging and is wrong. We need to be aware of the language we use.

*V'ahavta L'reiacha Kamocha* (**Love Your Neighbor as Yourself**): This is fundamental to Judaism. It starts with loving ourselves. If we wholly love and accept who we are, we gain the ability to extend that love and genuine acceptance to others.

*Al Tifrosh Min Hatsibur* (**Solidarity**): We all need to be part of a community. We should never isolate ourselves, even if we feel that we are different from others. We all need to find allies and friends to support us in our times of trial. And when we see someone struggling, we should strive to be that ally and support for them.

It's these lessons that I've learned through the Jewish culture that I treasure the most. It's knowing that what I do matters and that I have a real responsibility to make a difference for someone else. It's my hope that if I can see the world just a little bit differently, and share that perspective with others, maybe someone else will see the world a little bit differently too.

I don't look at Judaism and believe that everyone should be Jewish. We all have our own belief system, and people should believe what they want to. For me, Judaism isn't only about what I believe; it's about the values I hold dear and has everything to do with the importance of family and repairing the world.

Judaism has taught me that I need to respect everyone for what they believe and for who they are. I hope that others will respect me as well. Being Jewish has allowed me to appreciate the world and its people. The world is full of differences, and it's those differences that make us stronger.

## THE WORLD THROUGH MY CHILDREN'S EYES

When Noah and Mili were little, they really wanted to share the same room.

"Okay," I said, "we will put your beds in the same room, and you can share a room. But if you don't sleep, I will have to split you back up."

"You can't split us up!" Noah said defiantly. "We're twins!"

"Yeah! Twins!" Mili repeated.

I had to laugh at their response, and it has warmed my heart ever since. My Asian boy and Ethiopian girl saw themselves as twins. And they weren't afraid to fight for that title. That's just how my kids see the world. Wouldn't it be great if adults could see the world in the same way?

To be perfectly honest, I think that every child sees the world differently. When they act weird about something, it's usually because an adult has told them that something's not okay.

When Jacob was little, he was playing on the playground with a little boy who obviously had gone through some kind of chemotherapy or cancer treatment. He had lost most of his hair, with just patches of hair remaining on his head. When I asked Jacob if the little boy was okay and mentioned his hair, Jacob's answer was, "What are you talking about? We were just playing. He was really nice." He didn't even notice the hair until I said something. Children are innocent, and that is how they see the world. They don't judge; they just love.

That doesn't mean they don't see things. They may have a conversation that goes something like this:

"Oh, your skin's really dark. Why's it so dark?"

"Well, because I'm black."

"Oh, okay. Wanna play?"

There's no judgment there, just curiosity. And yes, that's a real conversation that Mili had on the playground. Wouldn't it be nice if adults could communicate with such simplicity and innocence?

When Mili was in preschool, I used to braid her hair in tiny little braids. The kids always wanted to touch her hair because some of them hadn't seen hair like hers before. She was the only black girl in her class. One day I was at school and one of the moms said, "My daughter has been asking and asking if you could braid her hair like Mili's." It was so endearing to me. If we could only be as innocent as a child, the world would be such a better place.

My own children get it. They see each kid in our family as unique and different, not because of their skin, but because of who they are. My children know they are valued and each of them have an important place in our family.

To me, one of the greatest blessings of my children is that they own who they are. And when they do talk about their color, it's always with pride or humor.

One day I bought Ari a black T-shirt. He put it on, and I told him how good he looked in it. He responded by peeling the shirt off and saying, "I always look good in black."

My children understand that the world we live in is a diverse world and that we need to appreciate that diversity. We have tried to teach them to reach outside of what is comfortable to them and really experience all the diversity the world has to offer.

If you create your own little world that is only centered on one thing, and only surround yourself with people who look, think, and act like you, you are missing out on so much good that you could be doing, and so many lessons you could be learning. We should appreciate all the differences.

I'm certain that many people will look at our family and see black, white, and Asian. But we don't see ourselves that way. We see our family as our family, and it's diverse because of what each person brings to the family, how we interact and respect one another. Our diversity isn't only because of the color of our skin. I'm not saying that we're color-blind, because we're not. We see color, and we appreciate the color, but that's just one part of our diversity.

We're diverse because of our thoughts, our ideas, our characteristics, our qualities, our likes, and our dislikes. In that sense, every family is diverse, and each family member is a unique and necessary part of the family. Families don't have to match. They just have to love each other and sometimes drive each other crazy. I believe this is part of the dictionary definition of family.

Our family is built on love. That is what makes our world go 'round. It doesn't matter where they came from, or the color of their skin—I love all my children with all my heart. That is the only thing that matters. When we told my dad we were adopting, he said, "I can be a grandfather to any child.

It doesn't matter where they're from. Every child needs to be loved." I've heard those words repeated over and over again in my mind. They're true for all of us.

The world is filled with diverse people, and all we really need to do is to love them.

## TOLERANCE VERSUS ACCEPTANCE

I often see a bumper sticker that says, "Tolerance. Believe in it." It's a symbol glyph that incorporates nine symbols including the peace sign, a gender equality sign, and different religious symbols. It depicts so much, but every time I see it, there's something about it that just doesn't resonate with me.

I think that we need to go beyond tolerance. In my opinion, to tolerate somebody is not positive. To tolerate somebody is like you're just putting up with them. You're not learning anything about them, and you're not trying to understand who they really are or why they do the things they do. You are just tolerating them. If I ever said to someone, "Oh, I tolerate you," it would be a complete insult!

Don't get me wrong; there's never a time when we shouldn't tolerate people. But to me, tolerance is not a positive message. A better message is that we need to accept others and to respect our differences. The bumper sticker I would like to see on more cars is ACCEPTANCE.

It is a shame to me that people struggle to accept another human being. We are all human, and every human should be accepted and respected. If we are judged, it should be on our actions, not on who we are or what we look like. It would be such a change for the world if we started really holding people accountable for their actions instead of their differences in appearance or belief.

I'm a firm believer that words matter. And it's important that we use our words wisely. Tolerance lacks the one thing that the world needs most—love. Acceptance and respect is a message filled with love and dignity. That's the message I want to champion.

## BE YOUR OWN AUTHENTIC SELF

Sadly, we live in a world right now where anti-Semitism is on the rise and intolerant people are walking into places of worship and shooting others because of their religion. Racism is rampant. We see it in healthcare, education, and even among some of the men and women sworn to protect us. The recent events with George Floyd, Breonna Taylor, Ahmaud Arbery, and Rayshard Brooks have made us more aware of the level of brutality against people of color and have brought us to a new level of consciousness regarding the penetrable fear that exists for black men and women as they attempt to live out their daily lives.

I've never wanted to hide from anything. I've always been proud of who I am, and I want my children to always be proud of who they are, too. Even still, with anti-Semitism, in addition to having children who are black and Asian, in a synagogue where there are very few Jews of color, our family is unique both in society and among our friends. I love the fact that we've added to the tribe. But for my children, I recognize that being a minority in both ethnicity and the Jewish culture isn't always easy.

We are proud of being Jewish. We are proud to have a multicultural family. Even when times are difficult, we have to choose to put ourselves out there, to stand up for the things we believe in and value, and to talk about making changes because that is the only way that change is going to happen. Even when the world seems scary, stand up for what's right, and don't be afraid to be who you are.

When I was a kid, Christmas time was hard because our neighbors always had a big, beautiful tree and there were Christmas lights everywhere. I always longed to have a Christmas tree, and it had nothing to do with religion. It had everything to do with sparkle and glitter and flashing lights. I can see my Jewish friends gasping as they read this.

When my children came to me and begged to decorate the house, I decided that I was going to figure out how to connect it to Hanukkah. I went online and found a plastic tree that looked like a leafless bush and I bought it. We call it our burning bush. We cover it with lights and hang Jewish ornaments (which I'm sure is an oxymoron) on it. We have menorah lights that we hang up around the house, and we decorate the house beautifully. Not because we're celebrating Christmas, but because we're celebrating Hanukkah, and because we wanted traditions of our own.

When the kids were younger and brought home ornaments that they had made at school, we would hang them on our burning bush, because what else could we do with them? We needed a place for them. For us, it was about celebrating our children and our family and togetherness. Those are the things that have always mattered the most to all of us.

Even within the realms of religion, I've learned that I need to be my own authentic self. The way I practice religion may be different than the way someone else does it. But I can't let the fear of being different stop me from being who I am.

I feel so strongly that in whatever we do, we need to do it in the way that's best suited for who we are, while allowing others the same privilege to express themselves exactly the way that's right for them. We need to stop judging one another and celebrate the differences. Respecting people for how they do things is important, even if they do things much differently than you.

## GET OUTSIDE THE BOX

Being Jewish has given me the community and values that have allowed me to live a life full of meaning. The values I've learned from Judaism have been the driving force of all the good I've been able to do. They've steered my journey and directed my path. They've taught me the dignity and value that can be found in every living soul.

My view of the world is bigger and brighter than it would have been without Judaism and the values I've come to love.

This may not be everyone's view of the world, but this is my view of the world, and it has helped me to be more open-minded and much less judgmental.

There are differences all around us. We're thin or curvy, short or tall, dark haired or blonde, Christian, Jewish, Muslim, Buddhist, Atheist—but the real truth is that we're all human. And we all have value. We've got to stop putting ourselves in a box of what we think each person should be, because we're all outside of the box. We're all unique.

My journey with Judaism and adoption has taken me outside of the box of societal norms. What I've realized from this perspective is that if more people stepped outside of the box that they define themselves by, they would recognize that there's really no box at all. We keep ourselves boxed up because of what we think we need to be, without realizing we have put ourselves, and others, in a box of our own making.

We each have just one life to live. We can live our best life when we learn to embrace the diversity that life has to offer, step outside of the box, and start truly living the life we have been given.

## IF YOU CAN MAKE A POSITIVE DIFFERENCE—DO IT!

Mother Teresa once said: "There are no great deeds, only small deeds done with great love."

We live in a world where so many of us want to make a difference, but as I've said throughout this book, making a difference doesn't require grand gestures and a deep pocketbook. It's the little things that we do that make a huge impact.

Mother Teresa changed the world caring for one person at a time. Remember, you don't have to change the world—just your small corner of it.

For forty-eight years, I've lived an amazing life full of ups and downs and chaos and comedy. But I never thought that by creating my family and doing what I love, I would inspire others to think about the paths they have chosen. I struggled for a long time to realize that I'm capable of inspiring those around me. I struggled to see my value. Trust me, it's not that I don't have self-confidence. But to realize that my life is inspirational to others takes it to an entirely different level. Now that I've realized this, it's my desire to use my words and my example to make a difference in my corner of the world. And I'll be thankful every day for the opportunity.

When you show up as yourself in the world, the world that you're able to change the most is your own. And—like ripples in a pond—"you being you" also changes the world of those around you. Every small positive action causes a ripple effect that can make a really big difference.

A woman at a gas station saw a man walking by her with a huge smile on his face. He wasn't even looking at her, but his smile changed her day. It was contagious and reminded her of the value of a simple smile. Sometimes it's the smallest actions that have the biggest impact.

Everywhere I go, I try to do my part in changing the world around me. When riding an elevator where everybody has awkward silence, I'll say hello to every person who gets in the elevator. We don't have to live in awkward silence and pretend that the other people aren't there. It's the strangest thing to me that when people get in an elevator or on a plane, they don't make eye contact or say a word to one another. We need to acknowledge one another, smile, give a word of encouragement, and brighten one another's day.

We can change the world—one person and one smile at a time.

I'm sure there are some who believe that a simple smile isn't a big deal and that it really can't do any good. But I disagree. You never know when someone you pass by is aching for someone to notice them, or to give them a simple word of encouragement. It just might be enough to truly change their day, and even their life.

There once was a teenager who cleared out his locker because his plan was to go home and kill himself over the weekend. But another teenager saw him struggling to carry his books as he walked home from school and asked if he could help. That simple act of kindness changed his whole path in life. That teenager who wanted to end his life is now a successful adult. There are people all around us who are struggling to just get through the day, and they are hoping for someone to notice them and to reach out in love, just as Mother Teresa did. If you have the opportunity to reach out to someone, do it. You will never regret it.

Looking back at my life, I don't think there's ever been a point when I've done something good and regretted my decision. Doing good for others has always made me feel good. I truly believe doing good will do the same for you.

## WE ALL HAVE THE SAME TWENTY-FOUR HOURS

Everyone has priorities. We have to live that way, or we would never get the important things done. But I have found that oftentimes we set things as priorities that really don't have to be, and then we use the excuse that we don't have time to do anything else. We can't go out there and help others, because we just don't have time for it.

This kind of scenario reminds me of my kids. They'll tell me that they don't have time to study for a test, and then I'll catch them watching a video on their phone. If they have the time to watch a video, they have time to study for their test. It's simply a matter of eliminating distractions and using time wisely.

We have the time to do so many good things. But a lot of our time is used up in distractions that really don't get us anywhere or have any positive effect on our life, or the world around us. Our time is about choices. We all have the same amount of time in a day, and if we really want to do something, we can do it. We just have to make that choice and make the time.

Working together with other people, figure out a way to make the time to accomplish the things you feel driven to accomplish. With your priorities in life, there are going to be things that other people can help you with so that you can do all the things that you want to do. But you have to choose to want to do them. You have to be willing to ask for help, and you have to be willing to share your vision with others.

We all have just one journey through this life. And regardless of the amount of time we've been given, we can spend it with our heads down, or we can choose to look up and see the world and the diverse people who surround us. We can choose to reach out with our hearts as well as our hands.

Despite the differences, each of us is left with the same question in this life: What will your journey be?

# CONCLUSION

The one thing I hope you take from this book is that you recognize just how extraordinary you are, and how your life is anything but ordinary. You are doing good, every single day, without even knowing it. The smiles you give, the meals you make, the doors you hold open, the words of encouragement you give, are all making a difference to the people you are doing them for.

Once we each become aware of the good that we are already doing in the world and recognize that even the little things we do can make a really big difference, we can intentionally make the choice to smile more, encourage more, love more, and to live more for others. That is how we can change the world.

My journey has taught me that this life, and finding our path in it, is about making choices. And every day, the small and seemingly inconsequential choices we make can change the world, starting with our own corner of it.

This life is all about the journey. It's never really about the destination. Just because you don't see the finish line, doesn't mean you should throw your hands in the air, give up, and stop moving forward. Life isn't about reaching the finish line; it's about all the things that happen along the way. It's about putting one foot in front of the other and taking one step at a time into an unknown world of possibilities. It is about climbing difficult mountains and finding the strength to keep moving forward. It is about discovering your own journey and owning your own path. Whether it's in your work, the work you want to do, or the work you do within the walls of your own home in developing and strengthening your own family—your journey is valuable, it is specific to you, and it is taking you exactly where you need to be.

### SHARE YOUR STORY

You are extraordinary just by being you. Remember that. Recognize the value you bring to the world and the good that you can do by sharing who you are. Your journey is as unique as you are, and by sharing your story, you have the ability to lift and strengthen others in ways you never thought possible.

By telling people about your life—your trials and triumphs— your story will influence others in a positive way. It will help them to realize those hidden things about themselves that they haven't yet discovered. And, most of all, it will help them find the value in themselves and the desire to discover their own journey. When we open up and share who we are with others, we realize that we are not alone and that there are others who are struggling with the exact same things that we are. We can be there for one another, to listen, to lift, and to strengthen each other for the journey ahead.

There will be difficult days for each of us in our journey. We may even have difficult weeks, months, or even years. Life is often hard, and moving forward isn't always easy. When we open up and share our weaknesses, as well as our strengths, our story can have a positive effect on others with similar difficulties in their own journey. Imagine the good we can do as we choose to see the good in our difficult situations and inspire others to do the same. Imagine the lives we can touch and the families we can strengthen. It all comes down to our choices—choosing to see the good around us and choosing to share it with others.

## MAKE A CHOICE

When we learn that our journey is built upon choices, we can look back and see how our choices have defined our journey.

Every choice that I have made has led me to something even greater than I could imagine.

I've run multiple half-marathons. I've climbed Kilimanjaro. I have hiked the Inca Trail. In addition to adopting, fostering, and being a leader, these things have shaped my journey and taken me to places I never dreamed of. But they all began with one simple choice.

Adoption was a choice. Running those marathons was a choice. Climbing Mount Kilimanjaro was a choice. Hiking the Inca Trail was a choice. And being a leader with the Jewish Federation was a choice.

I have traveled on missions all over the world, something I would have never imagined. I have spoken on many stages because of my volunteer work, and now I have written a book. It all started when a friend invited me to go to a meeting, and I said yes. The life I live now would have never happened if I would have said no to that simple invitation. Everything is interconnected. Even one small decision in one singular moment can take you down a completely different path. My own journey is evidence of that.

When those opportunities come knocking—say yes. Don't even hesitate, and don't be afraid to make a change. Let go of the fear and excuses, and jump all in. Because when you do, something extraordinary will happen—you will find your path and discover your journey.

So many of us mistakenly believe that our choices are only about the moment we are in. But looking back, we can see that every choice has brought us to where we are today, and without them, our life would have taken a totally different direction. Each choice, built upon the one before it, makes up the direction of our life and journey and affects every lesson that comes from it.

Although my choices have defined my journey, it is the lessons that have come from those choices that have brought meaning and direction to my life. It is my hope that by sharing those lessons and stories with you throughout the pages of this book, I have brought inspiration and direction for your own journey.

So many lessons, and so much goodness, has come to me in my life. But the lessons and goodness are always mixed and mingled with trials and hardships that are often difficult to carry. But as Mary Tyler Moore said, "You can't be brave if you've only had wonderful things happen to you." We need to experience the sorrow so we can better appreciate and value the joy. How we choose to meet and react to those hardships is the greatest lesson we can learn in our journey. This book was also meant to inspire you to know how to face life's challenges and keep moving forward in your journey.

## TREASURE THE LESSONS

Here are the twenty lessons I hope you remember:

Lesson #1: Be authentic. Don't try to be someone else. My dad used to always tell me, "Just be you." Now that he's no longer with me, those words are forever engraved in my heart.

Lesson #2: Whatever you are doing in life, the work is never done. It's about learning to appreciate the moments that you're in.

Lesson #3: Failure is necessary. Because we're human, everyone will fail at something. Learn the valuable lessons that come from your failure, and use them to make you stronger. Then keep moving forward in your journey.

Lesson #4: Don't compare. You can never walk in someone else's shoes. Every child is different, and so is every person. Stop comparing them to each other. And while you're at it, stop comparing yourself to others too.

Lesson #5: It's not what you're going through; it's how you react to it. You have the ability to see the good in every situation. It's a choice. Exercise that choice and find the good.

Lesson #6: Always lead with humor. There will be days when rats will total your minivan. Learn to laugh at yourself. Life can be ridiculous sometimes—laughter is the best medicine.

Lesson #7: Remember that it's okay to be human. Nobody is perfect, so stop expecting perfection from yourself and others.

Lesson #8: Life isn't always fair. There will always be challenges. It's how we face those challenges that will make the biggest impact.

Lesson #9: You don't have to change the world, just your corner of it.

Lesson #10: You can question people's actions, but not who they are. We all have value; look for the value in others, and find that value in yourself.

Lesson #11: When you have a choice, choose to be kind—and you always have a choice.

Lesson #12: Say YES! You don't have anything to lose by saying yes to something. And never use fear as an excuse to stop you from doing it. You may think you can't, but you really can.

Lesson #13: Be all in. In whatever you choose to do, jump in with both feet. Own who you are and every decision you make.

Lesson #14: You're not alone. We all have mountains to climb, but life is much easier when we choose to make that journey together. Find your people and embrace them as family.

Lesson #15: You create your own reality. No one directs your journey, but you. You are in the driver's seat, and you determine your path.

Lesson #16: Each person is a leader in their own way. We each have an influence on those around us. When we become more aware of how we can lift and strengthen others, we can do so much good and create a ripple effect of change.

Lesson #17: It's okay to have a different perspective than someone else. You don't always have to agree with others, but you should always respect them.

Lesson #18: Our world is diverse. Embrace that diversity and celebrate it. It's less about how we are different, and more about realizing how we are the same and how we must respect one another.

Lesson #19: Your journey is about choices. Choose to be the good. We have one life to live. Make it a good one.

Lesson #20: You are extraordinary exactly the way you are. Your journey matters, and so do you.

## BE THE GOOD

We each have a journey—even in our seemingly ordinary lives, we can do extraordinary things. Recognize the extraordinary things that you're already doing, especially for those you love. And wherever your journey takes you—always choose to be kind.

We're all human and we'll all make mistakes, but it's in our mistakes that we learn life's greatest lessons. Life may be hard at times, but as we push through, we can do those things we thought were impossible to us. Through small and simple steps, and with the help of those around us, we can conquer every mountain. Through patience, positivity, nonjudgment, and kindness, we can do so much for the world around us.

We have one life to live. Make it the very best life possible. See the extraordinary in your everyday life, and recognize the good you bring to the world, simply by the choices you make and the kindness you show. And when you're faced with a choice, go all in, and be the good.

# ACKNOWLEDGMENTS

I want to thank my husband, Rob, for being the most supportive man and offering up the best story material a woman could hope for. You are the only man who could put up with my "crazy."

Jacob, for being my first born and my test subject. You turned out really amazing despite my lack of a handbook.

Emma, for always being kind. Your daily phone calls while away at school always made me happy, even when I seemed distracted, aka not listening.

Olivia, for constantly needing a hug and for always being my sounding board. Your honest "advice," your extreme use of adjectives, and your amazing editing skills will be sorely missed as you move on to college.

Ari, for being so easygoing. You rarely complain and always step up when I need you the most.

Noah, for opening my eyes to a bigger world. You have taught me patience, love, and the ability to function on a minimal amount of sleep.

Mili, for always having a comment to every statement I make. You are strong, you are thoughtful, and you make me a better person.

My kids, as a tribe, for your patience, for your stubbornness, and for being amazing. I feel so lucky, almost each and every day (okay, every day), that I get to be your mom. You have each shown me the power of love and understanding.

Everyone I included in my stories—you make my world a better place.

Those who read my manuscript—your feedback was so valuable to me.

My closest friends—you put up with my lack of responses to text messages and phone calls because you knew I was just trying to get my work done. Your patience and lack of frustration with me is more than anyone could ask for.

My sister, Michelle—although sometimes I tried to act like the older sister, you will always be my big sister.

My mom, for teaching me the value of strength, resilience, and the importance of hard work. I will always look up to you.

And finally, I want to thank my dad. May his memory be for a blessing. He taught me that true love can conquer even the most stubborn of people. I will miss him forever.

# ABOUT THE AUTHOR

**SIMONE KNEGO** began her career as an accountant in 1995 working in Tyler, Texas. She moved to Sarasota, Florida, in 2000 and went back to school to become a teacher. Simone worked as an elementary and exceptional student education teacher for three years until she founded a medical device distributorship. Simone holds both a bachelor of science in accounting and a master's in accounting from the University of Florida and is a Certified Public Accountant.

Simone was the 2018–2019 Co-Chair of the Jewish Federations of North America's National Young Leadership Cabinet, the premier leadership development program of The Jewish Federations of North America. Simone just completed a six-year term serving as a board member of the Sarasota-Manatee Jewish Federation and was the 2016 Doris Loevner Memorial Young Leadership Award winner.

In 2015, she climbed Mt. Kilimanjaro to raise funds and awareness for the Livestrong Foundation. She has traveled on several philanthropic, international missions, including medical missions with her husband, Rob, who is a neuro-surgeon. They have been married for twenty-seven years and have six children.

Simone has led an ordinary life filled with extraordinary moments. As a wife, mother to six children (and three dogs), and a serial entrepreneur, she often splits her time between her family, businesses, and personal growth. She's realized that the small choices she makes every day to do good actually have the power to inspire others. Simone has shared this message with numerous audiences and, in doing so, has discovered her passion for public speaking. As she enters this next phase of her career, Simone hopes that her book, *The Extraordinary UnOrdinary You*, will inspire you to embrace life's ups and downs and realize the impact you're making on the world.

CPSIA information can be obtained
at www.ICGtesting.com
Printed in the USA
FSHW010414011020
74330FS